Bed & Breakfast
Alaska Style!

7th Edition — 2001-2002

by
Jan O'Meara

<u>**On the Cover:**</u>

FRONT — Sunset from Bluff House B&B, p. 65

Inset — Log House at Capt. Bligh's Beaver Creek Lodge, p. 81

Cover design by Ashley Huston

ISBN: 0-890692-03-4

Wizard Works
P.O. Box 1125
Homer, AK 99603

Contents

Welcome!

...to the 7th Edition of *Bed & Breakfast Alaska Style!* Whether this is your first look at us or you're an old friend, you will find in these pages some of the finest country inn and bed and breakfast establishments Alaska has to offer, including 18 new listings for this edition. You'll also find some scrumptious recipes to whet your appetite.

As you know if you've visited before, and as you will discover if you're traveling here for the first time, Alaska has a lot to offer its visitors. Among its special qualities are spectacular scenery, magnificent wildlife, fabulous fishing opportunities, and some of the friendliest folks you'll find anywhere. Alaskans enjoy sharing their love for this beautiful state, and many people who come as strangers depart as friends. Some even decide to make Alaska their homes.

The bed and breakfast accommodations listed in this book are as unique and diverse as Alaskans themselves. They run the gamut from single rooms in family homes to luxurious and elegant suites, to rustic cabins in the woods.. Some have ties to Alaska's historic past. Others are as new as today. But they all share the Alaska spirit that will make your visit memorable.

Whatever you're looking for, we'd like to help you find it. Come stay with us. You're as welcome as welcome can be!

— Jan O'Meara

ABOUT THIS BOOK

The following credit card abbreviations have been used throughout the book:

AMEX — American Express   CB — Carte Blanche
DC — Diner's Club   DS — Discover
MC — Mastercard   VISA — not abbreviated

Some Alaska communities charge bed taxes or other local taxes on accommodations. Unless otherwise indicated, the prices given in this book do not include those local taxes.

Prices given were current as of Fall 2000. Since prices are always subject to change, be sure to check these details with the B&B hosts before making plans.

Statewide
Reservations

Interior
Fairbanks •

Southcentral
Anchorage•

Southwest
Dillingham •

Southeast
Juneau •

ALASKA PRIVATE LODGINGS
STAY WITH A FRIEND

P.O. Box 200047
Anchorage, Alaska 99520-0047
(907) 258-1717; Fax (907) 258-6613
E-mail: apl@alaskabandb.com
Web site: www.alaskabandb.com

Hours:
9 a.m. to 7 p.m. in summer
variable winter hours
Credit Cards: AMEX, MC, VISA

Range of Rates:
Lower, $60-$75
Moderate, $76-$95
Higher, $96-$114
Luxury, $115 plus

Alaska Private Lodgings is a reservation service for Bed and Breakfasts, suites, private accommodations and cabins throughout the state of Alaska and the Yukon. They can save you time, dollars and many phone calls by reserving just the right accommodations to meet your needs. They have inspected all their properties and offer quality accommodations.

Alaska Private Lodgings promises you'll find comfortable, clean accommodations and an easy and convenient Alaska with local directions, dining suggestions and sightseeing recommendations provided by friendly hosts. Bed and Breakfast travelers are treated more like welcome guests than paying customers. A B&B is not just a place to stay, but an opportunity to meet local residents, enjoy people with common interests, and learn about sights and specialties known only by Alaska sourdoughs.

The service also makes reservations for transportation and select activities that are popular choices for the visitor to Alaska. The staff has the expertise to help plan individualized itineraries. You tell them what you're thinking about, and they recommend places and activities that best meet your needs and choices.

For a sampling of some of their properties, check out their web site.

Deposit and Refund Policy: Deposits will be refunded with 96 hours cancellation notice. Cancellation 96 hours or less prior to arrival date or "no show" will forfeit one night's accommodation rate.

Southcentral
Alaska

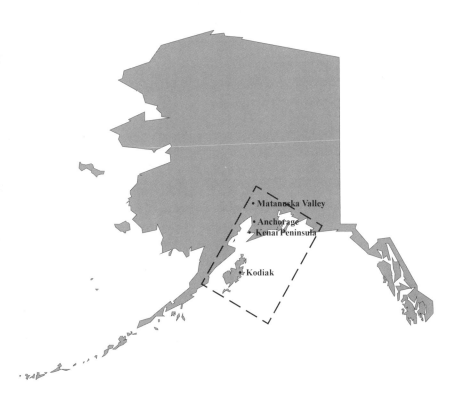

- Matanuska Valley
- Anchorage
- Kenai Peninsula
- Kodiak

Southcentral Alaska

Anchorage Area

- Anchorage
- Chugiak
- Eagle River
- Girdwood/Alyeska

Kenai Peninsula

- Homer
- Kenai
- Ninilchik
- Seward
- Soldotna

Kodiak

Matanuska Valley

- Palmer
- Talkeetna
- Wasilla
- Willow

Southcentral Alaska

Southcentral Alaska is home to nearly half the people who live in Alaska, and most of those reside in the Anchorage and Matanuska Valley areas.

Anchorage is the metropolitan heart of the area, and as you move away from the hub, the communities grow smaller and more intimate, and at the same time, the scenery seems to grow increasingly large.

The most diverse of Alaska's regions, Southcentral Alaska contains everything from coastal rain forest to mountain tundra, from urban malls to pristine wilderness. The area is crowned with spectacular mountains, including at least four sporadically active volcanoes. It is bordered along its southern end by the marine waters of the Gulf of Alaska, Resurrection Bay, Kachemak Bay, Cook Inlet and Turnagain Arm. At its northern edge, Mount McKinley (called Denali by locals) and its "mate" Mt. Foraker loom in majestic grandeur, marking the entry to Interior Alaska. Within its boundaries are three state parks, two national parks, two federal wildlife reserves, a brown-bear sanctuary and a national forest, as well as Alaska's largest city.

Because of its diversity, Southcentral Alaska offers visitors an amazing array of recreational opportunities. For those who enjoy getting out on the water, there are many rivers, lakes and bays in which to canoe and kayak. The waters offer abundant opportunities to fish for any of several species of sport fish, including the mighty king salmon and gigantic halibut. There are numerous hiking trails and camp sites in the area's several federal and state forests and parks. Mountain climbers can take their pick of any number of challenging peaks, from 14,163-foot Mt. Wrangell to the granddaddy of them all, 20,320-foot McKinley. Those who prefer to relax while others do the "work," have their choice of a myriad of sightseeing, flight-seeing and marine-touring options. And the more "culturally" inclined will be delighted by the variety of art galleries, museums, theater groups and musical and dance concerts to be enjoyed here.

Anchorage

Anchorage began its existence as a tent city back in 1915, when the Alaska Railroad was being built. It has come a long way from those humble beginnings. Today it is Alaska's largest city. As such, it boasts the same amenities as may be found in any large city — shopping malls, movie multiplexes, restaurants of all sizes and varieties, a major performing arts center, tall buildings and a cosmopolitan atmosphere. So citified is it now that some folks like to joke that it is only half an hour away from Alaska. But lest you think it too tame, it is also home to scores of wandering moose and the occasional foraging bear.

Anchorage is accessible by air, road and cruise ship. The Alaska Railroad also connects the city to Denali National Park and Fairbanks, in the Interior, and to Seward on the Kenai Peninsula.

Among the many things to do and see in Anchorage are:

☒ *Anchorage Museum of History and Art* — Located at the corner of 7th Avenue and A Street, the museum features artwork by local, national and international artists and offers permanent exhibits on Alaska history and Native culture. The museum also hosts special exhibits, which add to its variety.

☒ *Alaska Native Heritage Center* — Alaska's indigenous peoples are celebrated in this 26-acre park. Here, visitors can learn about traditional and contemporary Native cultures, including Aleut, Alutiiq, Athabascan, Eyak, Tlingit, Haida, Inupiaq and Yup'ik cultures. The center features dance and storytelling performances, arts and crafts demonstrations, replicas of traditional dwellings and community houses, a wonderful video about the several Native cultures, the Hall of Cultures, and a gift shop.

☒ *Alaska Zoo* — The zoo, located on O'Malley Road in south Anchorage, is home to a wide variety of Alaska animals, including black, brown and polar bears, moose, musk oxen, caribou, owls, fox, wolves, eagles and sea otters. The zoo has become home to orphaned or abandoned animals, such as its elephant, Siberian tiger and lynx.

☒ *Biking and Hiking Trails* — There are 120 miles of paved bike trails in the Anchorage bowl, including the Chester Creek Greenbelt and the Coastal Trail. The Greenbelt trail winds along the creek's edge from east Anchorage to Cook Inlet, where it hooks up with the Coastal Trail. The Coastal Trail skirts the Inlet from downtown Anchorage to Earthquake Park. Either trail makes an easy walk. For more serious hikers, there are numerous trails into Chugach State Park from the Hillside or Turnagain Arm area. Check with the Park office for maps.

☒ *Golf Courses* — Russian Jack Park, off DeBarr Road in east Anchorage, not only contains some lovely picnic and hiking spots, it boasts a 9-hole golf course as well. Fort Richardson and Elmendorf military bases allow public access to their 18-hole courses. There is another public 18-hole golf course on O'Malley Road.

☒ *Fine Dining* — Whatever your taste in food, chances are you'll be able to satisfy it in Anchorage. Numerous restaurants specialize in a variety of fresh Alaska seafood, as well as such other Alaska delicacies as reindeer sausage and reindeer stew. Ethnic choices include Thai, Chinese, Japanese, Korean, French, Greek, Italian, Mediterranean, and Mexican. Several restaurants offer a unique gourmet dining experience which may or may not feature Alaska specialties. There are also a number of steak houses and a wealth of fast-food chain restaurants.

☒ *Log Cabin Visitor Center* — This is the place to start if you want to know what's happening in Anchorage and where to find what you're looking for. Located at the corner of Fourth Avenue and F Street, the visitor center features maps, brochures and other information on Anchorage and surrounding areas.

☒ *Potter Marsh State Game Refuge*— About 10 miles south of downtown Anchorage, the refuge is an important nesting place for waterfowl. A boardwalk winds from the parking lot out over the marsh, giving visitors a chance to view close up lesser Canada geese and their offspring, a variety of ducks, Arctic terns and, in spring and fall, trumpeter swans.

ALASKAN FRONTIER GARDENS
BED & BREAKFAST

P.O. Box 241881
Anchorage, Alaska 99524-1881
(907) 345-6556; Fax (907) 562-2923
E-mail: afg@alaska.net
Web site: www.alaskafrontiergardens.com
Rita Gittins, Hostess

Months Open: Year-round
Hours: 24
Credit Cards: VISA, MC, AMEX, DS
Accommodations: 3 rooms

Children Welcome: All ages
Pets Accommodated: Yes
Social Drinking: Yes
Smoking: Outside

ROOM RATES*
Ivory Suite
Summer: $150 single; $195 double
Winter: $100 single; $150 double
Garden Terrace
Summer: $125 single; $165 double
Winter: $85 single; $100 double
Fireweed Room
Summer: $75 single; $100 double
Winter: $60 single; $75 double
(*Weekly and off-season rates are available)

An elegant, spacious home near Chugach State Park on Anchorage's

peaceful Hillside, just 20 minutes from the airport and downtown, Alaskan Frontier Gardens is in a scenic, wooded neighborhood at the corner of Hillside Drive and Alatna. Inside a wooden fence, the home sits nestled among trees, lawns and

flowers, making this the ultimate location for a refined hideaway. Alaska Frontier Gardens offers a museum-like environment with Alaskan hospitality, which combines a warm and relaxing atmosphere with exceptional comfort. Hostess Rita Gittins is a true Alaskan with an active and well-traveled knowledge of Alaska, enjoying many interesting hobbies, including hunting, fishing and sightseeing.

Hiking, horseback riding, golfing, swimming or visiting the Alaska Zoo are just some of the things to do in this beautiful area of town. Alaskan Frontier Gardens B& B can provide seasonal and sporting accommodations for many other activities for the true Alaskan adventure.

Alaskan Frontier Gardens' *Ivory Suite* is exquisite, with inviting amenities that include a private bath, king-size bed, fireplace, cable TV, VCR, sauna, large multi-person Jacuzzi, double shower and view. The *Garden Terrace Room* has a private bath, king-size bed, cable TV, VCR and double Jacuzzi with hanging plants. The *Fireweed Room* offers a spacious shared bath with a double and single beds and cable TV. Guests are welcome to use the barbecue grill and outdoor hot tub. This is the ultimate location and meets every expectation for a getaway, honeymoon or weddings.

Breakfast here is absolutely heavenly. Guests awake to the aroma of gourmet breakfast delights that may include special-recipe Belgian waffles with rum peaches, Amaretto French toast, reindeer sausage, fresh-ground gourmet coffee, tea, home-baked pastry, fresh fruit, hot and cold cereals and juice.

"At our bed and breakfast, we feel our warm and friendly Alaska hospitality and service is very important and probably is the reason we have many returning guests and personal references," Rita says.

AURORA WINDS B & B RESORT

7501 Upper O'Malley
Anchorage, AK 99516
(907) 346-2533; Fax (907) 346-3192
E-mail: awbnb@alaska.net
James Montgomery, Host

Months open: All year
Hours: 24
Credit cards: VISA, MC, AMEX, DS
Accommodations: 5 suites

Children welcome: Yes
Pets accommodated: Inquire
Social drinking: Yes
Smoking: In designated areas

ROOM RATES
Single: $95+ summer, $55+ winter
Double: $135+ summer, $75+ winter
Each additional person: $25

Aurora Winds is an elegant bed and breakfast resort located on two secluded acres in Anchorage's Hillside area, just 12 minutes from the airport and 15 minutes from downtown. At Aurora Winds, guests are only three minutes from world-class cross country skiing and downhill skiing areas, horseback riding, golf, tennis, the Anchorage Zoo, Chugach State Park and nearly 1/2 million acres of fine Alaska wilderness.

Guests have their choice of five suites, each with private bath, TV, VCR and telephone. The *Mountain View Suite* features traditional furnishings, a queen-size bed, and a deep Kohler soaking tub. *The Southern Com-*

fort Suite features contemporary furnishings, a queen-size canopy bed, trundle bed, and vanity desk. *The Copper Suite* is furnished with contemporary and oriental furnishings and features a solid copper queen-size sleigh bed, twin silk chaise, and kitchenette. The *Garden Suite* has Scandinavian furnishings, a queen-size bed and a twin bed. There is also access to an expansive deck from this suite. *The McKinley Suite* is a luxurious 800-square-foot unit, featuring a sitting area with fireplace, solid cherry queen-size sleigh bed and queen-size sofa bed, and a double Jacuzzi and steam shower in the bath.

As if all this weren't enough, Aurora Winds boasts an exercise room with full gym and sauna, a billiard room, theater room, four fireplaces, two family rooms and an eight-person hot tub outside under the stars.

For breakfast, guests have their choice of full or continental, brought to their door or served at table.

Host James Montgomery is a 27-year veteran of the hospitality industry, educator and service professional. He and his mini long-haired dachshund will make your stay at Aurora Winds a pleasant one.

Bananas Foster AM

3 c. Krusteaz Pancake/Waffle Mix
2-1/2 c. HOT water
1/2 c. Caramel flavoring

1 T. cinnamon
1/3 c. chopped pecans

Mix above ingredients and make waffles as usual, then top with following:

2 firm ripe bananas, sliced
2 T. butter
2 T. brown sugar
1 dash cinnamon

Touch of nutmeg
2 oz. Amaretto
2 oz. brandy

In a flambe pan, combine butter, sugar, cinnamon and nutmeg. Stir constantly while heating, until a thick sauce has formed. Add bananas and stir until they are coated evenly. Increase flames under the pan and add brandy and amaretto. Tilt pan to allow flame to light the liquor. Stirring constantly, burn off all the alcohol, then ladle bananas and sauce over top of waffles. Serves eight.

Cheney Lake Bed & Breakfast

6333 Colgate Drive
Anchorage, Alaska 99504
(907) 337-4391, (888) 337-4391; Fax (907) 338-1023
E-mail: cheneybb@alaska.net
Web site: www.alaska.net/~cheneybb
Mary Kluis and Janetta Pritchard, Hosts

Months Open: 12
Hours: Check-in 3 p.m., out 11 a.m.
Credit Cards: MC, VISA
Accommodations: 3 rooms

Children Welcome: No
Pets Accommodated: No
Social Drinking: Yes
Smoking: Outside

ROOM RATES
Single: $95 summer, $50 winter
Double: $95 summer, $50 winter
Each additional person: $20

Located in a quiet neighborhood on Cheney Lake in East Anchorage, this lovely home looks out on the lake and has a beautiful view of the Chugach Mountains. The home is comfortable, with Alaskan decor and many artifacts.

Each room, which overlook the lake, has a private bath and is furnished with king-size bed, TV, VCR, and telephone. Candies, nuts and a carafe of cold water are provided in each room. Guests are welcome to use

Bed
&
Breakfast

the outdoor hot tub, where they can soak in comfort while watching the ducks and geese on the lake.

In the living room, guests can curl up beside a nice warm fireplace and watch their choice of videos on the 48-inch television.

Mary, a teacher in Anchorage, has lived in Alaska since 1981. She was born and raised in Minnesota. Janetta was born and raised in Alaska. She works for the State of Alaska as a land manager. The two share their home with one small dog, who is old and not tolerant of small children.

Breakfast is continental and may consist of muffins, bagels with cream cheese, juice, milk, coffee, tea and fruit. The menu varies each day.

The Anchorage Botanical Garden is a mile from the house, and is filled with beautiful Alaska flowers and plants. A pathway around the lake and the nearby bike path offer plenty of walking opportunities.

Copper Whale Inn

440 "L" Street
Anchorage, Alaska 99501
(907) 258-7999; Fax (907) 258-6213
E-mail: cwhalein@alaska.net
Web site: www.copperwhale.com

Tony Carter, Innkeeper; Angelique Joseph, Manager

Months Open: 12
Hours: 8 a.m.-5 p.m., but guests accepted at all hours
Accommodations: 18 sum.; 13 wint.
Children Welcome: Yes
Pets Accommodated: No
Social Drinking: Yes
Smoking: No
Credit Cards: MC, VISA, AMEX, DC, JCB

Room Rates
Shared bath: $120 summer, $65 winter
Private bath: $125-$165 summer, $79 winter

In one of the most convenient locations in town, Copper Whale Inn sits at the corner of 5th Avenue and L Street, right next to the downtown business and shopping area. The inn, the historic Romig House and new addition, has ties to Anchorage's earlier days. In summer, guests may be housed here, or in the Elderberry Park annex, the Oscar Anderson House. Both the inn and the annex offer Beluga Whale watching opportunities from most rooms.

The Copper Whale Inn is decorated in a clean and bright Nantucket style and is surrounded by flowers, ponds and fountains. Overlooking Bootleggers Cove, it offers some spectacular views of Cook Inlet, the Alaska Range and Mt. Redoubt and Mt. Spurr volcanoes. There is a comfy common room area with a gas fireplace.

There are 14 guest rooms at the inn. In the main house, two upstairs rooms, furnished with queen beds, share a bath and a half bath; the remaining six rooms have private baths. Five of the rooms have queen-size beds, the sixth has two twin beds. The new edition has three rooms with queen size beds and three with queen-size beds and full-size futon beds. All have private baths.

There is a loading zone in front of the inn, on L Street, but the only parking is across the street. It costs $9 for 24 hours.

The annex, located only a block away from the inn, has on-site parking. It is a two-story house with four guest rooms, all with private baths, and an on-site host. Three of the rooms offer queen-size beds and a twin, and the fourth is furnished with a double bed. The house is very quiet, and the deck overlooks Cook Inlet.

Breakfast is served buffet-style in the common room, but the kitchen area is manned at all times. Guests may have their choice of cereal, fresh fruit, yogurts, assorted breads, pancakes, waffles, bacon, sausage, ham and cheese croissants, milk, orange juice, and assorted coffees, teas and chocolates. Cookies are baked daily and are available for snacking.

Innkeeper Tony Carter is a marine biologist who formerly taught at the Seattle Aquarium and the University of the Philippines in Hiloilo City. He also managed the Main Bay Hatchery and served as assistant manager of the Esther Island hatchery in Prince William Sound. Manager Angelique Joseph travels extensively about Alaska and has a working knowledge of the state. The rest of the staff keeps updated on what is going on so they can help guests who have questions. "We are all helpful," Tony says.

The inn and annex are within walking distance to museums, art galleries, shops, restaurants, as well as the federal and state courthouses. Only a short distance away, guests can hire a horse-drawn carriage for a short tour of the downtown area. Anchorage's popular Coastal Trail is also nearby, offering plenty of opportunity for biking, walk-ing, or in-line skating. Tony also offers "Killer Tours" for $65 a person, from 9:30 a.m. to 4 p.m. daily. These tours are based in Tony's well-spring of knowledge about marine biology and include stops at the Ship Creek Weir and State Hatchery or Potters Marsh, a drive along Turnagain Arm, with a stop at Beluga Point, and then on to Portage Glacier and, finally, to Big Game Alaska.

ELDERBERRY BED AND BREAKFAST

(By the Airport)
8340 Elderberry
Anchorage, Alaska 99502
(907) 243-6968; Fax (907) 243-6968
E-mail: elderberry-b-b@gci.net
Web site: www.alaskan.com/elderberrybb
Norm and Linda Seitz, Hosts

Months Open: Year-round
Hours: 24
Credit Cards: MC, VISA
Accommodations: 3 rooms

Children Welcome: All ages
Pets Accommodated: Kenneled
Social Drinking: Yes
Smoking: On deck

ROOM RATES
Single: $70-$90 summer, $60 winter
Double: $70-90 summer, $60 winter
Each additional person, $10; Children, $10 extra

Close to the airport and bike and walking trails, Elderberry Bed and Breakfast is in the Sand Lake area of Anchorage. It is close to the bus route and within walking distance of several popular restaurants. The Seitz's home is a two-story comfortable yellow house with traditional furnishings and Alaskana accents. Linda and Norm take special pride in their yard and

flowers in the summer. Linda has won blue ribbons when she shows her flowers. Often moose can be spotted from the large viewing windows in their sun room. There are three guest rooms. One has a double bed with private bath across the hall, and is decorated in Victorian pale green and rose. Another room has a queen-size bed with shower in the room, and is decorated in green and white wildflower design. The third room has a queen-size bed and twin bed, private bath, and is decorated in lemon yellow and marine blue, with a nautical design.

Guests are welcome throughout the main level of the home and may choose to sit by the fireplace in the sitting room and read from Alaska books. Guests are also welcome in the sun room to sit by the woodstove, watch videos or TV, or chat. Both Norm and Linda have lived in Alaska since 1977 and love to meet new people and share their Alaska experiences with them. Linda considers Norm one of their most popular amenities, as he loves to talks with their guests.

Linda and Norm will cater to your needs and will try to fill any request, from a special diet to parking for your RV (they provide parking space, complete with electricity and water hookups). They will provide freezer space for your catch as well as a TV in your room.

Linda makes a full breakfast, which may include oven omelettes or quiches, hot homemade bread with homemade strawberry jam and a fresh-fruit compote.

ELDERBERRY B&B COFFEE CAKE

Coffee cake

1/3 c. margarine	1/4 tsp. salt
1/3 c. sugar	1/2 c. buttermilk
1 egg	**Topping**
1/2 tsp. vanilla	1/4 c. brown sugar
1 c. flour	1/4 c. finely chopped nuts
1/2 tsp. soda	1/4 c. coconut
1/2 tsp. baking powder	1/4 tsp. cinnamon

Cream together first two ingredients. Add remaining ingredients and mix Spread batter in greased 8" round cake pan. Sprinkle batter with the topping. Cover and refrigerate overnight. Next morning, bake at 350° for 20-25 minutes. Serves 6.

THE OSCAR GILL HOUSE
HISTORIC BED & BREAKFAST

1344 West 10th Avenue
Anchorage, AK 99501
Reservations: (907) 279-1344; Fax (907) 279-1344
E-mail: oscargill@gci.net
Web site: www.oscargill.com
Mark and Susan Lutz, Hosts

Months open: 12	**Children welcome:** All ages
Hours: 24	**Pets accommodated:** No
Credit Cards: AMEX, MC, VISA	**Social drinking:** Yes
Accommodations: 3 rooms	**Smoking:** Outside

ROOM RATES
October-April, 2000-2001: $75 all rooms
May-September 2001: Single, $85;
Double, $95 (shared bath), $110 (ensuite bath w/jacuzzi)
Each additional person, $20

Walking into the Oscar Gill House is like stepping back into history, but with all the modern conveniences. The house, which is featured in *The Official Guide to American Historic Inns*, was built around 1913 by Oscar Gill, Iditarod mail carrier, three-term Anchorage mayor and Speaker of the Territorial House. In 1993 it was moved to Anchorage and thoughtfully

renovated by hosts Mark and Susan Lutz, in cooperation with Anchorage Historic Properties. It is furnished throughout with appropriate antiques for a simple and homey decor.

The house is located on the Delaney Park Strip, mere blocks away from downtown Anchorage. The Performing Arts Center, museum, courthouse, microbreweries, gourmet restaurants and shops are all within walking distance. The railroad and airport are only minutes away. Complimentary bicycles and skis allow guests to take advantage of the nearby Coastal Trail. City basketball and tennis courts are close by.

There are three guest rooms, each privately keyed. Room 1 contains a queen-size bed and a twin bed, a private bath with a jacuzzi, and cable TV. Room 2 has a double bed and shares a bath with Room 3, which features a queen-size bed. The bath is graced by a claw-foot tub and shower. Body Shop toiletries and robes are provided. Other amenities to enhance your homestay experience include laundry facilities, good books, good magazines, and good company. Hostess Susan Lutz is justifiably proud that for the fourth year this B&B has been praised in *Frommers Alaska* as one of the "best B&Bs in Alaska," receiving the coveted * that designates this as a favorite spot, not to be missed.

A full breakfast is served by Susan, and might include blueberry buttermilk pancakes or sourdough French toast, eggs, orange juice, fruit, coffee and assorted teas.

There is a 14-day cancellation policy. Refunds, minus a $15 cancellation fee, are subject to the room being re-booked.

1915 TENT CITY CAKE

2 c. sugar	1 t. baking powder
2 c. strong coffee	1 t. cinnamon
2 c. raisins	1 t. cloves
1 med. apple, peeled & shredded	1 t. allspice
2 c. flour	1 t. nutmeg
1 c. chopped nuts	1 t. baking soda

Simmer sugar, coffee, raisins and apple for 10 minutes. Cool 10 minutes. Mix dry ingredients and add to cooled sauce. Bake in a 9" by 13" pan at 350° for 20 minutes. Can be frosted.

THE LILAC HOUSE

950 P Street
Anchorage, AK 99501
(907) 278-2939; Fax (907) 278-4939
E-mail: lilac@pobox.alaska.net
Debi Shinn, Host

Months open: 12	**Children welcome:** Yes
Hours: Check-in 3 p.m., out 11 a.m.	**Pets accommodated:** No
Credit Cards: MC, VISA, AMEX	**Social drinking:** Yes
Accommodations: 3 rooms	**Smoking:** No

ROOM RATES
King Suite w/private bath: $135 summer, $95 winter
Queen Room/Twin Room, shared bath: $95 summer; $75 winter
Each additional person: $25

The Lilac House is located in a quiet, well-established residential area across from the Delaney Park Strip, within walking distance of downtown restaurants and shops. The house was originally built in the 1950s, with an addition in 1979. The bed and breakfast area was added in 1989. The present owners purchased the home in 1996 and reopened the bed and breakfast in 1997.

The bed and breakfast area is reached through a separate entrance, with a security lock that is programmed with a code for each guest on the day of arrival, so they are guaranteed access any time after check-in. The

guest rooms are on the second floor of the home and share a common kitchen area, with refrigerator, microwave and a full complement of dishes and cookware. An iron and ironing board are available.

Each guest room has a private telephone line and answering machine. The King Room contains a king-size bed, sofa, private bath, vaulted ceilings and opens to a deck that has a view of Cook Inlet, Mt. Susitna and the Alaska Range. The Queen Room features a queen-size bed, built-in desk, a rocking chair, and opens onto a deck which faces Delaney Park and the Chugach Mountains. It shares a bath with the Twin Room, which has two twin beds, a built-in desk and a sitting area. It also opens onto a deck facing the park and mountains. Terrycloth bathrobes, slippers and hair dryers are provided.

A continental breakfast is set up in the newly added breakfast room between 7:30 a.m. and 10 a.m. and guests can help themselves at their convenience. Breakfast includes fresh baked bread, muffins or sweet bread, fresh fruit, assorted hot and cold cereals, biscotti, assorted juices, coffee and a selection of teas. During the summer, fresh flowers grace the table. Guests who have early morning planes or trains to catch are provided with a "to-go" breakfast.

Debi is a former secondary loan underwriter, who resigned after 16 years to devote her time to running The Lilac House. Besides running the B&B, Debi likes to cook, play golf, hike, cross-country ski and travel. She shares her home with two cats and a big, friendly Bouvier dog, Tango. The animals are not allowed in the guest area.

RHUBARB BREAD

1-1/2 c. brown sugar	1 tsp. soda
1 egg	2 c. chopped rhubarb
2/3 c. oil	1/2 c. nuts
1 tsp. vanilla	**Topping**
1 c. buttermilk	1/2 c. sugar
2-1/2 c. flour	1 T. soft margarine
1 tsp. salt	1/2 tsp. cinnamon

Mix together sugar, egg, oil, buttermilk & vanilla. Add salt, soda and flour. Fold in rhubarb and nuts. Pour into two greased loaf pans. Combine topping ingredients and sprinkle over top. Bake at 350° for 60 minutes.

MAHOGANY MANOR
204 East 15th Avenue
Anchorage, Alaska 99501
(907) 278-1111; Fax (907) 258-7877; Toll free 888-777-0346
E-mail: mahoganymanor@compuserve.com
Web site: www.mahoganymanor.com & www.bedandbreakfast.com
Mary Ernst and Russ Campbell, Hosts

Months Open: 12	**Children Welcome:** Yes
Hours: Check-in 5-7 p.m., out 11 a.m.	**Pets Accommodated:** No
Credit Cards: MC, VISA, AMEX	**Social Drinking:** Yes
Accommodations: 4 rooms	**Smoking:** Outside only

ROOM RATES
October 2-April 30: single or double, $129; suite, $159-229
May 1-September 30: single or double, $189; suite, $229-$289
$25 per additional person; $10 surcharge for one-night stays

Perched atop a bluff overlooking the Chester Valley green, historic Mahogany Manor continues to charm visitors with its unique blend of comfort and elegance. Designed for entertaining and social events, it was the venue for numerous gala affairs for prominent Alaskans and visiting dignitaries during the 1960's and 70's. The facility boasts over 2000 square feet of richly appointed lounge area, two grand fireplaces (one of which is a 6 foot wide copper hooded fire pit), numerous waterfalls, swimming and

outdoor whirlpool facilities and impressive panoramic views of the surrounding grounds, city and mountains through its floor-to- ceiling windows. Add to this the convenient location at the edge of downtown Anchorage and you have the perfect lodging choice for the discriminating visitor.

Each guestroom at Mahogany Manor is unique, private and comfortable. In-room amenities include telephones, robes, slippers, hair dryer, make-up mirror, iron, cable TV, VCR and high speed internet connection, a complete toiletries basket and Alaskan chocolates.

The *Northern Lights Room* is furnished with a king size bed that can be converted to two twin beds upon request. It has a two-room bath, with a shower and toilet in one room and a sink and mirror in an adjacent area. This guestroom is on the main level, with the guest kitchen and entry nearby, and is accessible without stairs.

The *Governor's Suite* is a large, three-room suite with two private bedrooms and a common sitting area. The private ceramic tile bath has a shower and a double vanity. The sitting area has a wall of sliding glass doors to the south that overlooks the surrounding woodlands. A wall of windows to the north overlooks the courtyard with an abundance of trees and raised flowerbeds (during growing season) and downtown skyline beyond. This suite is also accessible without stairs. In the winter, this suite is

converted to the two-room *Sourdough Suite* for the convenience of business travelers.

The *Royal Suite* is a luxury suite on the lower level and is accessed by following the floating, solid oak circular staircase. A white brick fireplace complements the room interior of redwood walls and ceiling. The spacious bath offers a tub, separate extra-large shower and large double ceramic tile vanity. The separate dressing area has an abundance of mirrors. As the manor is built into a hillside, this suite also has a panoramic view of midtown and the surrounding woodlands. From September 1 to May 15, a minimum four-night stay is required for this suite. The room can accommodate up to two rollaway beds.

The *Cabin* offers quiet seclusion on the lower level. As with the *royal Suite*, it too is accessed down the oak staircase. A private bath, with ample counter space, tub and shower is located adjacent to the room. This guest room has two walls of windows with blinds that offer the maximum in privacy, but also allow guests to enjoy the outdoor views.

A hearty continental breakfast is available anytime in the guest kitchen. Breakfast fare includes choice of breads and pastries, hot and cold cereals, yogurt, fruit and/or fruit juices, coffee, tea, milk and hot chocolate.

Whirlpool and swimming facilities are available to overnight guests in the summer free of charge (at specified posted hours) and at an additional charge during the winter.

Hosts Mary Ernst and Russ Campbell have lived in Anchorage for more than 30 years. Both enjoy traveling and sharing information about Alaska with guests. Mary, a Certified Travel Counselor, has worked in the travel industry for more than 30 years and has experience in both leisure and business travel. Russ has engineering experience in the Alaskan oil industry and with state and federal government. They share the facility with a small dog that can be confined to the owner's living area when requested.

Mahogany Manor is just minutes from downtown shops, restaurants and businesses, near ski and bike trails and only a half-mile from the Sullivan Arena and Mulcahy Park. Also, the "People Mover" city bus route is only two blocks away.

There is a 14-day cancellation policy. A $25 processing fee applies to all cancellations. Reservations are guaranteed with the first nights deposit; with the balance due 14 days before arrival in summer, and 7 days before arrival in the winter.

MOOSEWOOD MANOR

Box 113188
Anchorage, AK 99511-3188
(907) 345-8788; Fax: (907) 345-2188
E-mail: moosewd@alaska.net
Web site: www.alaska.net/~moosewd/
Lowe-Page Family, Hosts

Months open: 12
Hours: 24
Credit cards: MC, VISA
Accommodations: 3 rooms

Children welcome: w/supervision
Pets accommodated: No
Social drinking: Discouraged
Smoking: No

ROOM RATES
Single/Double: $108-118 summer; $88 winter

This distinctive bed and breakfast is nestled in the heart of 400 undeveloped acres in the Rabbit Creek Valley, adjoining Chugach State Park in the south Anchorage Hillside area. Guests can enjoy a 360-degree view of the mountains and valley, and across Cook Inlet to the Alaska Range, while knowing they are only 20 minutes from the airport, downtown Anchorage, and the Alaska Railroad depot. The Anchorage golf course and Alaska Zoo are only five minutes away.

The exterior of the home features contemporary earth and copper colors. The interior features clean, contemporary lines and quiet, Zen-like elegance. The facility is designed to accommodate a variety of special needs, including wheelchair access, low vision and respiratory needs.

Accommodations are spacious, with room for meetings, seminars, weddings and workshops of up to 30 people. Outdoors, there is room for several hundred guests.

There are three bedrooms, each with a queen-size bed, private bath, TV, VCR and telephone. Each is furnished with natural-fibre linens and towels. Two of the rooms and one of the baths is wheelchair accessible. The *Rabbit Creek Room* bath includes a Japanese soak tub.

Other amenities include fax and copy availability, robes and hairdryers, handmade soap, mints on the pillow, free local telephone calls, laundry facilities, library, videos, board games and wildlife viewing from all windows.

A self-serve buffet, which features hot and cold cereals, breakfast breads, fruit, juices, yogurt, smoothies and hot drinks, is available from 7:30 a.m.-10 a.m. Vegetarian gourmet specials are prepared and served daily, between 8 and 9 a.m. All food is fresh, organically grown, and garnished with flowers and herbs grown at Moosewood.

Hot drinks are available 24 hours a day. A bread and cheese platter is provided in the evening. Popcorn, fruit and cookies are also available.

The Lowe-Pages are longtime Alaskans who love to travel, are avid gardeners, and are knowledgeable about Alaska art and anthropology.

SWAN HOUSE BED AND BREAKFAST

6840 Crooked Tree Drive
Anchorage, Alaska 99516
(907) 346-3033, (800) 921-1900; Fax (907) 346-3535
E-mail: swan1@alaska.net
Web site: www.alaskaswanhouse.com
Judy and Jerry Swanson, Hosts

Months Open: Year-round	**Children Welcome:** No
Hours: 6 a.m. – 10 p.m.	**Pets Accommodated:** No
Credit Cards: MC, VISA	**Social Drinking:** Yes
Accommodations: 3 rooms	**Smoking:** No

ROOM RATES
Single: $149 summer $129 winter
Double: $169 summer, $139 winter

Swan House Bed and Breakfast overlooks the city of Anchorage, with a view of Mt. McKinley in the background. It is in a quiet, hillside neighborhood with lots of trees and moose, 15 minutes from town or airport. *Travel & Leisure* magazine dubbed it "one of the best places to stay in Anchorage" and called it a "trophy home."

Swan House is architecturally unique, with 127 windows and more wood than you will ever see in a home. The exterior is heartwood redwood.

Oak dominates the interior with a black walnut and Corian fireplace. Corian is in every room, as are antiques from all over the world. The home has been the setting for numerous weddings and honeymoons.

Swan House has three guest rooms with private baths, one with a queen-size bed, and one with a king-size bed or two twin beds. All rooms have cable TVs and phones.

Jerry and Judy Swanson are both pilots and fly the food and supplies to their Seldovia B&B weekly. Jerry is retired from the FAA, and Judy has been an air traffic controller with the FAA since 1978.

Guests may expect full gourmet breakfasts with fruit smoothies, fresh-ground coffee and tea. Beverages are available any time.

Area activities include hiking, biking, cross-country and downhill skiing and golfing (one mile from the house).

ALMOND CROISSANT FRENCH TOAST

Mix together with a beater:
6 eggs
1/2 c. cream or milk

1/2 c. almond syrup (espresso-type)
1 tsp. cinnamon

Cut frozen croissants in half, sandwich-style. Dip in batter quickly. Put on heated griddle (400°). Flip when browned. Put on plates and sprinkle with powdered sugar and sliced almonds.

Serve with bacon or reindeer sausage and honey-butter syrup. Serves 8.

WALKABOUT TOWN
BED AND BREAKFAST

1610 "E" Street
Anchorage, Alaska 99501
(907) 279-7808; Fax (907) 258-3657
E-mail: tstimson@compuserv.com
Web site: www.travelguides.com/bb/walkabout/
Sandra and Terry Stimson, Hosts

Months Open: May 15–Sept. 15	**Children Welcome:** Yes
Hours: Check-in, 4 – 7 p.m.	**Pets Accommodated:** No
Credit Cards: VISA, MC	**Social Drinking:** No
Accommodations: 3 rooms	**Smoking:** Outside on decks

ROOM RATES
Single: $60
Double: $75
Each additional person: $15

Walkabout Town Bed and Breakfast is located a short walking distance from downtown and 10 minutes from the airport. This convenient home offers friendly, knowledgeable hosts, a full breakfast after 7:30 a.m., free use of bicycles for the Coastal Trail, and occasional free rides to the railroad station.

As indicated by the name, this bed and breakfast is within walking distance of the Anchorage museum, the log cabin visitors center, the downtown shopping mall and other tourist attractions. For those who would rather ride, two buses pass by almost every hour.

Hosts Sandra and Terry Stimson are retired educators. Sandy is a docent at the Anchorage museum. Terry is a former Alaska state senator.

Sandy loves to cook, and each morning at 7:30 she prepares an all-Alaska breakfast that features sourdough waffles, reindeer sausage, rhubarb or berry syrup and other Alaskan flavors. A continental breakfast is available for early risers.

Accommodations include a variety of bed accommodations to meet the needs of two, three or four people desiring to share a room. Two rooms share a bath. The *Russian Room* has a king-size bed. The *Australian Room* has a queen-size and a twin bed. The *Piano Room* features a queen-size bed and twin beds.

THE YORKSHIRE
BED & BREAKFAST

8511 Pioneer Drive
Anchorage, Alaska 99504
(888) 701-8499; Fax (907) 337-9564
E-mail: YorkshireB-B@GCI.net
Web site: home.gci.net/~yorkshireb-b
Joe and Maryann Lisenby, Hosts

Months Open: 12   **Children Welcome:** Yes
Hours: Check-in 5 p.m., out 10 a.m.   **Pets Accommodated:** No
Credit Cards: MC, VISA   **Social Drinking:** Yes
Accommodations: 1 room   **Smoking:** Outside only

ROOM RATES
Single: $65 winter, $75 summer
Double: $75 winter, $85 summer
Each additional person: $10

This home-style Bed and Breakfast is located just 20 minutes from the Anchorage airport or downtown and just 10 minutes from the military bases in East Anchorage. The home was built in 1975 and remodeled in 2000. It is decorated in Southwest style. An 800-square-foot deck offers

guests a wonderful place to relax and watch the wildlife that may stroll through the back yard. There is one bedroom, with a double bed and private bath. Bathrobes are available. A fruit bowl, coffee, tea and hot cocoa are in the room. Cold beverages are also available.

A full, hearty, homemade breakfast is served to guests, and may include pancakes, eggs, reindeer sausage, toast or muffins. Egg souffle and breakfast-in-a-glass are house specialties. Fresh fruit is always available, as are coffee, tea, hot cocoa and other beverages.

Laundry facilities and a hot tub are available. Bike and walking trails are nearby.

Joe and Maryann Lisenby came to Alaska in 1976 with two small children, to serve at Elmendorf Air Force Base. Both have since retired from the Air Force. They raised their two children in Anchorage and have enjoyed all that Anchorage and Alaska have to offer. They enjoy sharing their experiences with visitors. The couple shares their home with two Yorkshire terriers, for whom the B & B is named.

Eagle River – Chugiak

Starting about 13.5 miles northeast of Anchorage is a small string of communities which together form the city's most populous suburb. Eagle River, Chugiak and Peters Creek have long been a refuge for people who want to work in Anchorage but live in a more rural, relaxed setting. Eagle River is the hub of these communities and the site of numerous restaurants, shopping centers and gas stations. Its sister city, Chugiak, is home to the area's high school and junior high school. Among the area's attractions are:

☒ *Chugach State Park Visitor Center* — Chugach State Park was one of Alaska's first state parks, and it is a jewel. It runs along the Chugach Mountains behind Anchorage, from Eagle River to Turnagain Arm. The park is lined with hiking trails guaranteed to give spectacular views of the entire Anchorage bowl and beyond. The opportunities the park offers for wildlife viewing and photography are unparalleled. The visitor center can be found at the end of a 13-mile drive from downtown Eagle River along scenic Eagle River Road. The center has telescopes for wildlife viewing and offers ranger-led hikes and naturalist programs. It is open year-round.

☒ *Eagle River* — Adventurous spirits have their pick of class II, III and IV float trips on this beautiful river. Rangers at the Chugach State Park Visitor Center will give information on river conditions.

☒ *Eklutna Village Historical Park* — This park, centered in the traditional Athabaskan village of Eklutna, is home of the oldest building in the Anchorage area, St. Nicholas Russian Orthodox Church. In 1924, the U.S. Department of Interior established a home here for Native children orphaned by the 1918 influenza epidemic.

☒ *Southcentral Alaska Museum of Natural History* — The museum, which is located in the Parkgate building in downtown Eagle River, showcases indigenous wildlife and fossils from the surrounding mountains. Hours vary, so call 694-0819.

☒ *Visitor Information Center* — Located in the Valley River Mall in Eagle River, the center offers further information about things to do and see in the area.

PETERS CREEK
BED & BREAKFAST

22626 Chambers Lane
P.O. Box 670370
Chugiak, Alaska 99567
(907) 688-3465 or (888) 688-3465
Fax (907) 688-3466
E-mail: stay@peterscreekbnb.com
Web site: www.peterscreekbnb.com
Bob and Lucy Moody, Hosts

Months Open: Year-round   **Children Welcome:** Yes
Hours: 6 a.m. – 11 p.m.   **Pets Accommodated:** Inquire
Credit Cards: VISA, MC, AMEX, DS   **Social Drinking:** No
Accommodations: 3 rooms, 1 suite   **Smoking:** No

ROOM RATES
Single: $80
Double: $90
Each additional adult: $20
Children under 12: $15
Rates include full, hearty Alaska breakfast.

Centrally located between Anchorage and the Mat-Su Valley, this newly built bed and breakfast is located on the north shore of Peters Creek in the middle of two and a half wooded acres. King salmon spawn in the creek, which is the habitat for other fish as well.

"Our large spacious home is a smoke-free environment and has been designed with the physically challenged in mind," hosts Bob and Lucy Moody say.

The home is furnished predominantly with Victorian antiques. There is a fireplace in the living room and a large-screen home theater in the family room for guest use. A large recreation room with exercise equipment is also available for guests.

Each room is furnished with cable TV, VCR, refrigerator, iron and board, robes and slippers. All rooms have private baths and are theme decorated. The *Alaska Room* has a queen-size bed; the *Violet Room* has a queen-size bed. The *Field & Stream Room* is suitable for families, with two queen-size beds and enough room for a twin rollaway and crib if needed. The *Family Suite* includes the *Rose Room* and *Noah's Ark Room* for children, and sleeps six or seven. The suite has its own private bath.

Parks, swimming, skiing, dogsled rides, hiking, fishing and museums are all nearby.

EASY LOW-FAT STRAWBERRY CREPES

1 carton low-fat strawberry yogurt
fresh or frozen strawberries
powdered sugar
crepes (can be homemade or store bought)

Stir up yogurt and spread on crepes. Slice strawberries and place on top of yogurt spread. Roll up crepe and put on plate. Spread yogurt lightly on top of each crepe and top with more sliced strawberries. Sprinkle lightly with powdered sugar. Warm in microwave for 50 seconds (may vary according to microwave) — or, if your plates are oven-safe, warm in oven at 200°. Serve plain or with warm strawberry syrup.

Girdwood–Alyeska

Located 37 miles south of Anchorage, just off the Seward Highway, nestled in the arms of the Chugach Mountain Range, lies Girdwood. Girdwood began life as a mining community in the 1800s, but has evolved over the years into Alaska's largest downhill-ski area. Alyeska Resort offers several chair lifts, a luxury hotel and a number of fine restaurants. The ski lift operates year-round, for skiers in winter and sightseers in summer. An aerial tram takes visitors up to two mountainside restaurants. There is also a trail for hiking to the summit, and numerous cross-country ski trails for winter enjoyment. Biking, berry picking, gold panning, fishing, flightseeing and rafting make this area as enjoyable in the summer as in the winter.

Other visitor attractions in the area include:

☒ *Crow Creek Trail* — The trail offers an easy four-mile hike to Raven Glacier. Along the trail, hikers may see gold-mining relics, Dall sheep and a beautiful alpine lake. A longer, 25-mile, trail can be completed in three days, taking hikers along a portion of the historic Iditarod Trail. The longer trail follows the old mail trail, passing through Chugach State Park and ending at Eagle River.

☒ *Portage Glacier/Begich-Boggs Visitor Center* — The center, located at the end of Portage Glacier Road on the shore of Portage Lake, overlooks Portage Glacier, Alaska's most visited attraction. The center features natural-history exhibits, a 200-seat theater with daily films in the summer, an enclosed observation post, and guided hikes. Blue-white icebergs that have "calved" from the glacier dot the lake and are often blown close to shore by winds. A private concessionaire offers boat trips on the lake was formed by the melting of the glacier. The center is open daily from Memorial Day through Labor Day and on weekends from March to May and September through October.

☒ *Big Game Alaska* — This privately owned park offers visitors the chance to see Alaska wildlife outside of a zoo environment. Animals in the park include caribou, moose, elk, Sitka black tailed deer, bison and birds of prey. There is a picnic area and a gift shop for visitors' convenience.

ALYESKA VIEW
BED AND BREAKFAST

P.O. Box 234
Girdwood, Alaska 99587
(907) 783-2747; Fax: (907) 783-2747
Heinrich and Emmy Gruber, Hosts

Months Open: Year-round
Hours: Check-in after 4 p.m.,
check-out by 11 a.m.
Credit Cards: MC, VISA

Children Welcome: Over 6
Pets Accommodated: No
Social Drinking: Yes
Smoking: Outside

Accommodations: 3 rooms

ROOM RATES
Room A, king-size bed: $85 double
Room B, 2 full beds: $85
Room C, twin beds: $75
Each additional person: $15 & up
Single person: $75

Hosts Heinrich and Emmy Gruber moved to Alaska from Austria in 1964 and built their own home in Girdwood. Heinrich is a carpenter, Emmy,

a hairdresser. They both speak German and enjoy cross-country and downhill skiing and biking. Heinrich has trained for and run the Seward Mount Marathon race every year since 1979.

Alyeska View Bed and Breakfast is a two-story European chalet-style house surrounded in summer by many different flowers. The upstairs deck has a view of mountains and glaciers. Alyeska Ski Resort is within walking distance. It's a 15-minute drive to the Portage-Whittier railroad shuttle and a 20-minute drive to Portage Glacier.

Accommodations consist of three bedrooms with down comforters, a private entrance for guests, and a large shared bathroom with shower and Jacuzzi.

The Grubers serve a full breakfast with omelets, French toast, bacon and eggs or pancakes, juice, tea, coffee and homemade breads.

Reservations are preferred, but walk-in guests are welcome.

Kenai Peninsula

The Kenai Peninsula is one of Alaska's most popular recreation destinations. Located just an hour's drive from downtown Anchorage, it is a favorite locale for tens of thousands of visitors from Alaska and all over the world.

It is an area of supreme scenic beauty and unparalleled opportunities for wildlife viewing, fishing and boating, and it draws artists, photographers and fishermen like the proverbial magnet.

Besides its many rivers that run rife with salmon in the summertime, it boasts some of the most spectacular coastlines seen anywhere. Glaciers cling to its rugged mountains, volcanoes arc along its western rim, eagles soar through its clean, clear skies, sea otters, seals and whales swim along its shores. In the summer, woods, fields and shores shimmer with the life and color of myriad birds and wildflowers.

Some of Alaska's earliest European settlements began here, as trading posts and colonial villages set up by Russian fur traders nearly 200 years ago along the shores of Cook Inlet and Resurrection Bay. Some of the artifacts they left behind can be found in community museums in Homer, Kenai and Seward. The area traces its Native heritage to Dena'ina Athabaskan Indians and Sugpiaq Eskimos, whose descendents still live along its shores.

After the fur hunters came the gold seekers. They didn't find much, but they left their mark. Those who came later did find gold, black gold. Some of Alaska's earliest producing oil fields were found on the Kenai Peninsula and offshore waters. Drilling rigs still dot the waters of upper Cook Inlet, and can be seen from the communities of the northern peninsula.

Besides rich history and spectacular scenery, visitors to the area can enjoy museums, art galleries, dance and theatrical performances, and some of the best hiking, fishing and boating to be found anywhere in Alaska.

Homer

Homer is a vibrant community of artists, fishermen and others who enjoy living in what has been called the Carmel of Alaska. Roughly 220 road miles and 90 air miles from Anchorage, it nestles on one arm of a fjord, along the northern edge of Kachemak Bay, one of Alaska's richest marine environments. It boasts a five-mile-long natural spit, a healthy commercial and charter fishing industry, and a wealth of talented and productive practicing artists, whose work can be seen in local art galleries and gift shops.

Homer came to life at the turn of the century, when coal miners and gold hunters first sought to tap its riches. They were succeeded by fox farmers, homesteaders and fishermen. Then in the 1970s, the area began to blossom into one of Alaska's most prodigious art colonies. With a commanding view of deep blue waters, sparkling glaciers and magnificent mountains, it is easy to understand Homer's lure. The many things to do and see include:

☒ *Art Galleries* — Homer's many art galleries feature a wide variety of work created by local artists, as well as artists from other areas within and outside of Alaska.

☒ *Pratt Museum*— One of Alaska's finest museums, the Pratt houses a collection of artifacts from Kachemak Bay's earliest people, as well as the more recently arrived homesteaders and Russian Old Believers. Summer features include a live remote video camera that shows the birds of Gull Rock as they go about their daily lives. Another camera is stationed at the McNeil River Brown Bear Sanctuary, and visitors can watch the bears as they fish for salmon.

☒ *Pier One Theatre* — This excellent community theater company offers a full season of productions every weekend throughout the summer in its warehouse theater on the Homer Spit. It also sponsors the annual August performance of the Kenai Peninsula Symphony Orchestra.

☒ *National Maritime Wildlife Refuge Visitor Center* — The center offers information about the marine wildlife in the surrounding area and throughout the refuge, which extends through the Aleutian Islands.

COPPER HELMET B&B

P. O. Box 2604
Homer, Alaska 99603
(907)235-5608 or (800) 964-2991; Fax (907) 235-1975
E-mail: copper@xyz.net
Web site: alaska-homer.com
Dwight and Lana Simpson, Hosts

Months Open: 12
Hours: Check-in 4 p.m., check-out 11 a.m.
Credit Cards: MC, VISA, DS
Accommodations: 3 rooms

Children Welcome: Yes
Pets Accommodated: No
Social Drinking: Yes
Smoking: No

ROOM RATES
Single: $65 winter, $89 summer
Double: $75 winter, $98 summer
Each additional person: $15
Children: $10

Copper Helmet B&B is a one-level, ranch-style home located two miles out East Road, behind the American Legion Hall. The house is natural wood with white trim and has lots of windows, allowing visitors to enjoy the maximum impact of Homer's magnificent setting. There is a large common area for visitors' use, which includes a big screen TV/VCR, a deck and an outdoor hot tub.

Each of the three guest rooms has a TV and refrigerator in room, and a private bath. Bathrobes are supplied. The *Eagle Room*, which sleeps four, has a queen bed, twin bed and a rollaway. It is carpeted. The *Moose Room* also sleeps four. It has a California king bed and a set of bunk beds. The *Wolf Room*, also called the *Queen Room*, has a queen bed and sleeps two. These two rooms have hardwood floors.

Breakfast at Copper Helmet is full and hearty. It may include a main entree of eggs, French toast, or pancakes, and side dishes of ham, sausage or bacon, hash browns, home-baked coffee cake, muffins or pastries. Yogurt, fresh fruit, breads and bagels, and cereals are also offered, along with orange juice, coffee, tea or milk.

Hostess Lana Simpson was born and raised in Kodiak and moved to Homer in the late 1980s. Dwight came to Alaska in the late 1960s and moved to homer in the early 1980s. The couple opened their B&B in 1995. They have a daughter, age 8, and a friendly cat, called Tigger.

A 50% deposit or credit card is required to hold a room. Reservations must be cancelled 14 days in advance to avoid a charge to your card or to receive a full refund.

BERRY FRENCH TOAST

10-12 slices day-old French bread	1 16-oz bag frozen mixed berries
5 eggs, slightly beaten	1 c. sugar
3/4 c. milk	1 T. cornstarch
1 T. vanilla extract	1 T. pumpkin pie or apple pie spice
1/4 tsp. baking powder	1 T. cinnamon-sugar

Place bread slices in a large, shallow baking dish. Combine eggs, milk, vanilla and baking powder and pour over bread. Cover and chill 8 hours or overnight. Remove from refrigerator 30 minutes before baking.

In a bowl, combine berries, sugar, cornstarch and pie spice. Pour into a greased 9"x13"x2" baking dish. Arrange prepared bread on top. Sprinkle with cinnamon-sugar. Bake uncovered at 400° for 35-40 minutes.

FERNWOOD ESTATES B&B

P. O. Box 900
Homer, Alaska 99603
(907) 235-2070 or (888) 788-2838; Fax (907) 235-2838
E-mail: fernwood@xyz.net
Web site: www.fernwoodestates.com
Bob and Leah Handley, Hosts

Months Open: 12	**Children Welcome:** Yes
Hours: 24	**Pets Accommodated:** No
Credit Cards: VISA, MC	**Social Drinking:** Yes
Accommodations: 4 rooms	**Smoking:** Outside

ROOM RATES
Single: $55 winter; $85 summer
Double: $65 winter; $95 summer
Each additional person: $15
Children under 10, with own sleeping bag, free

Fernwood Estates B&B sits at the top of East Hill Road, on Cottonwood Lane, offering its guests a magnificent panorama of Kachemak Bay and the mountains and glaciers beyond. Capitalizing on its location, every room has a view, and there is a large wraparound deck for outside viewing and relaxing. The house also has an open, airy great room for lounging.

There are four bedrooms, each with a private bath and fabulous view. The *Leilani Room* has a floral decor, a jacuzzi tub, and a queen and twin

bed. The *Borealis Room* has a northern sky theme. It has a private deck and a queen-size bed. The *Chart Room*, decorated in a sea motif, has a queen size and a twin bed. The *Heritage Room* has handicapped access, its own private entrance, and a great view of the bay.

A full breakfast is served between 7 a.m. and 9 a.m. and may include reindeer sausage, a multi-ingredient omelet, French toast or blueberry-sourdough hotcakes. Freshly ground coffee, tea and juice are staples. "There's always more than guests can eat," Leah says. Occasionally, Leah also offers her guests an evening dessert, but cold crinks and coffee are always available.

Bob's family homesteaded in 1954, and he has great stories of Alaska's past to share with guests. Leah's been in Alaska 18 years. The couple has traveled to many parts of the world. They boast a very friendly atmosphere, with their two children as the resident entertainment.

KACHEMAK BAY ADVENTURE COMPANY
THE WATER'S EDGE
THE GARDEN HOUSE

P. O. Box 341
Homer, Alaska 99603
(907) 235-3772; Fax (907) 235-2230
Web site: www.kbayadventure.com
David & Pat Matthews, Owners

Months Open: May 1-Oct. 1
Hours:
Credit Cards: Yes
Accommodations: 2 2-bdr. houses

Children Welcome: Yes
Pets: On Approval
Social Drinking: Yes
Smoking: No

ROOM RATES
The Water's Edge: $300 per night, based on 4 or more people
The Garden House: $150 per night, based on double occupancy
Additional guests $25

The Garden House is a two-bedroom home on Bear Creek Drive, about two and a half miles east of Homer. The house has two decks, a large lawn, flower and vegetable gardens, and a raspberry patch that guests are welcome to use. The 1,100-square-foot house was built in the summer of 1999 and features vaulted ceilings, tile floors, a fully-equipped kitchen

with all new appliances, and a washer/dryer. There is a grill on the deck and a freezer available for guest use. Guests at the Garden House have easy access to all that Homer has to offer.

The house sleeps six or more people comfortably. The first level bedroom is furnished with a queen-size bed. The second level bedroom overlooks the living room below and is furnished with a king-size bed and two twin beds. The entry, kitchen, living room and bathroom are located on the first level. Rooms are light and airy and are decorated with original artwork.

The Water's Edge is located across the bay at Halibut Cove Lagoon, and is accessible by private boat, water taxi or float plane. There is a private gravel beach for easy landing and a mooring buoy and floating dock. A large, cedar-lined, wood-fired sauna is located at the beach, along with enough firewood for campfires and sauna. The 1,000-square-foot house is on a knoll overlooking the water, up a steep trail and steps.

The house can sleep ten or more people in a dormitory-type arrangement. Sleeping accommodations include a loft area that is furnished with a king-size bed and queen-size futon. The first level bedroom has a bunkbed with a full-size bed on the bottom and a twin-size on top. There are three twin-size foam mattresses, a foam pad on the windowseat and a couch that can be used for sleeping, as well. Extensive decks make ideal tent platforms for larger groups.

This is a more rustic accommodation, and guests are encouraged to bring their own sleeping bags, although some linens and towels are available on site for those traveling without such gear. Creek water is piped to the kitchen sink and should be boiled or filtered before drinking. There is no running hot water and no indoor bath. The outhouse is located downhill from the house and there is a cold-water shower in the sauna. The house is heated by a woodstove and there is dry firewood stored close by.

The Water's Edge is only about a 10-minute walk from the Kachemak State Park Ranger Station and the trailhead for 80 miles of maintained hiking trails. During May and June, schools of king salmon run right along the beach in front of the house. There is trout fishing in China Poot Lake, a 2.5 mile hike from The Water's Edge. Kayaks are available for those who would like to explore Halibut Cove Lagoon. Kayaking into or out of the channel leading into the lagoon is not advised due to strong tidal currents.

Breakfast at both houses is continental, self-fix, self-serve, from fixings provided, so guests can eat at their convenience. Some staples are also provided, such as flour and sugar. Popcorn is available for snacking.

Hosts David and Pat Matthews are long-time Alaska residents interested in natural history, gardening, hiking, sailing, fishing and skiing.

KACHEMAK KIANA BED & BREAKFAST

58856 East End Road
Homer, Alaska 99603
(907) 235-8824; Toll free 866-235-8824; Fax (907) 235-8349
e-mail: kiana@xyz.net
Web site: www.akms.com/kiana
Hosts Jerry & Lou

Months Open: April 1-October 31
Hours: Check in after 3 p.m.;
check out by noon
Credit Cards: None
Accommodations: 3 rooms, 1 cabin

Children Welcome: Older only
Pets Accommodated: No
Social Drinking: Yes
Smoking: No

ROOM RATES
Single: $80-$100
Double: $90-$110
Guest cottage (sleeps two): $120
Each additional person: $30
(Summer rates are given; inquire about winter rates,
in effect Sept. 16 through April 15.)

Kachemak Kiana Bed & Breakfast is a spacious, comfortable home with a panoramic view of Kachemak Bay, several glaciers, Kenai Mountains and the Homer Spit. The large living room has an open-beamed ceiling and a marble fireplace. Here, you can leisurely sit and enjoy the many views. A separate den also has a fireplace and a television. The kitchen is

available for coffee, teas and other snacks. Host and hostess Jerry and Lou live downstairs and are readily available to assist guests.

There are three roomy bedrooms at Kachemak Kiana, each with a private bath, large closets and comfortable furnishings. The master bedroom has a king-size bed and an oustanding view of Grewingk Glacier. The suite has a king-size bed with a private sitting room that looks onto the bay. The third room has extra-long twin beds and views a wooded canyon.

Completing the bed and breakfast is a small, two-story cottage located at the back of the property. It offers privacy, a queen-size bed upstairs, a deck off the bedroom, a full bathroom, and a small living room/kitchennette downstairs.

A large, cedar enclosed hot tub is available for all guests.

Kiana is located five miles from town on East End Road. Paved parking is ample. Often you might see a moose or a sandhill crane on Kiana's acreage. "Kiana" means welcome to this place.

Summer breakfasts include egg dishes, sourdough pancakes or French toast, with sausage or bacon. Cereals, fresh fruit, a freshly baked sweet, coffee, teas and juice are also available. In August, raspberries are abundant and available for picking.

KIANA RASPBERRY MUFFINS

1/2 c. butter, softened	2 c. flour
1 c. sugar	2 tsp. baking powder
2 large eggs	1/4 tsp. salt
1/2 tsp. almond extract	1/2 c. milk
2 c. raspberries	

Whip butter and sugar, add eggs and almond extract and mix well. Mix dry ingredients. Add the flour mixture, half at a time, alternating with the milk. Fold in raspberries. Fill muffin tins and top with sugar and cinnamon. Bake at 375° for 25 minutes.

Optional glaze: 1 tsp. almond extract
                    1 c. powdered sugar
                    Add milk to desired consistency

THE SHOREBIRD GUEST HOUSE

P.O. Box 204
Homer, Alaska 99603
(907) 235-2107; Fax (907) 235-5435
Rose Beck and Claudia Ehli, Hosts

Months Open: May 1-Labor Day
Hours: Until 10 p.m.
Credit Cards: MC, VISA
Accommodations: 1 efficiency guest house

Children Welcome: All ages
Pets Accommodated: No
Social Drinking: No
Smoking: No

ROOM RATES*
Two people: $120; $20 each additional person
Weekly rate: $700 for 1-3 guests, $750 for 4 or more
(* Prices do not include local taxes.)

The Shorebird guest House sits on the beach of Kachemak Bay, across the bay from Grewingk Glacier. This completely self-contained guest house has its own entrance and sports a modern decor. Full kitchen, bathroom, sitting and sleeping area all flow together with a four-window view of Kachemak Bay. The guest house has a queen-size bed, queen-size hide-a-bed and a full-size futon bed.

Among the many amenities offered at The Shorebird are cable TV, mountain bike rental, beach access, and shorebird, sea bird, seal and sea otter viewing.

Claudia and Rose are both long-time Alaskans, budding naturalists and birders. They offer their clientele interesting information about birds, fauna and flora.

Breakfast is not included, but the guest house has a fully equipped kitchen with pots, pans, appliances and dishes, and is stocked with coffees, teas and assorted meal preparation items. A baked treat welcomes guests on arrival. Visitor activities in the Homer area include deep-sea fishing, boat tours across the bay, the Pratt Museum, local artists' shops, fishing from shore, birding and beachcombing.

RANGER COOKIES

1 c. butter	2 c. flour
1 c. white sugar	1 tsp. baking soda
1 c. brown sugar	1 tsp. salt
2 eggs	1 c. rolled oats
1 T. vanilla	1 c. flaked coconut
2 c. Rice Krispies	1 c. chopped nuts

Blend butter and sugars together. Add eggs and vanilla. Mix remaining ingredients together and add to egg mixture. Drop on oiled cookie sheet in walnut-size pieces. Flatten. Bake at 350° for 8-10 minutes or until golden brown. Cool. These store well.

SKYLINE BED & BREAKFAST

63540 Skyline Drive
Homer, Alaska 99603
(907) 235-3832; Fax (907) 235-3832
Lisa & Karen Cauble, Hosts

Months Open: Year-round
Hours: 24
Credit Cards: VISA & MC
Accommodations: 4 rooms

Children Welcome: Yes
Pets Accommodated: On approval
Social Drinking: Yes
Smoking: Outside

ROOM RATES*
Single: $80; Double: $85; Queen: $95
King suite: $115 (2 night minimum stay)
Each additional person: $25
Will work with large families
*Call for winter rates

Located in a quiet wooded setting on Skyline Drive above Homer, Skyline Bed and Breakfast offers a beautiful view of Grewingk Glacier and Kachemak Bay. The large, beautiful home features four rooms with private baths, cathedral ceilings, Victorian decor and beautiful, handmade Victorian lamps in every room.

The *King Suite* has a private bath, a king-size bed, and is decorated in southern Victorian style. The *Wild West Room* contains a queen-size bed and a single twin bed, the *Sweetheart Room* contains a double bed. *Lisa's Room*, a sweet little room, has two twin beds and handmade quilts.

Other amenities include a children's play area, library, fireplace, and plenty of serenity. There is RV parking, and refrigerator and freezer space available.

Breakfast is continental and includes home baked goodies, fresh fruit, juices and hot beverages. On weekeneds, guests can expect extras like wildberry French toast. Snacks are available all day.

WILDBERRY FRENCH TOAST

1 loaf French bread, sliced 1"	1 16-oz. pkg. frozen mixed berries
6 eggs	1 T. cornstarch
3/4 c. milk	1 T. pumpkin pie spice
1 T. vanilla extract	3/4 c. sugar
1/4 tsp. baking powder	1 tsp. cinnamon

Place bread slices in large shallow pan. Combine eggs, milk, vanilla and baking powder. Pour over bread. Cover and refrigerate overnight. In the morning, remove from refrigerator. Combine berries, 1/2 c. sugar, pumpkin pie spice and cornstarch. Pour over bread mixture. Sprinkle with 1/4 c. sugar mixed with cinnamon. Bake at 400° for 30-35 minutes. Sprinkle with powdered sugar and serve.

SPRUCE ACRES
BED & BREAKFAST CABINS

910 Sterling Highway
Homer, Alaska 99603
(907) 235-8388 or (877) 500-7404; Fax (907) 235-0636
E-mail: sprucea@ptialaska.net
Web site: www.spruceacrecabins.com
John & Joyce Williams, Hosts

Months Open: Year round
Hours: 8 a.m. to 10 p.m.
Credit Cards: VISA, MC, DS
Accommodations: 4 cabins

Children Welcome: All ages
Pets Accommodated: Inquire
Social Drinking: No
Smoking: Outside only

ROOM RATES
Guest cabins: $60-$95 summer; $50-$70 winter
Each additional person: $15
Children under 5 years, with sleeping bag, free

Spruce Acres Bed & Breakfast has four cute and cozy cabins decorated in country/Victorian style. A creek and pond add to its "small farm atmosphere."

There are chickens to feed and ducks in the pond to feed. It's so relax-

ing to watch, parents love it as much as the kids. Each summer there are baby chicks and ducks hatching.

The cabins have private baths, homemade quilts and feather beds, color TVs, VCRs, phones, kitchenettes and living rooms. A barbecue pit may be used by guests. Alaska videos, a Nintendo game, laundry facilities, a portable crib and freezer space are available on request. RV parking is available.

The *Fireweed Cabin* has two bedrooms and sleeps five. It is furnished with a queen-size bed, single bed, and bunk beds. The *Lupine Cabin* has one room and is furnished with a queen-size bed. The *Wild Rose Cabin* has one bedroom and sleeps three. It is furnished with a double bed and a single bed. The *Forget-Me-Not Cabin* has two bedrooms, and sleeps five. It is furnished with a king-size bed and three single beds.

Coffee, tea and mocha are available in each cabin. Breakfast is self-serve and usually includes some kind of homemade bread, cinnamon rolls, banana bread or muffins.

Joyce and John have lived in Alaska for 30 years and have been hosting B&B guests since 1987. They have two dogs, a Lhaso apso named Nikki, and a poodle named Lacy. The dogs act as official greeters, and the cat, Sam, is happy to give a loving cat fix to guests who are missing their own pets.

The B&B is located on the Sterling Highway, just before downtown Homer. Wide sidewalks lead into town or up the hill to the Baycrest overlook, for Homer's most spectacular view.

SPRUCE ACRES MOCHA

Mix together:
1 c. hot chocolate mix   1 c. sugar
1 c. coffee creamer   1 c. instant coffee mix

Put 2-3 tablespoons in a cup, add hot water, stir and enjoy!

VICTORIAN HEIGHTS
BED AND BREAKFAST

P.O. Box 2363
Homer, Alaska 99603-2363
(907) 235-6357
E-mail: victorian_heights@hotmail.com
Web site: www.lodginghomeralaska.com/victorian.htm
Phil and Tammy Clay, Hosts

Months Open: May-September
Hours: 8 a.m. to 11 p.m.
Credit Cards: MC, VISA
Accommodations: 5 rooms

Children Welcome: Yes
Pets Accommodated: No
Social Drinking: No
Smoking: No

ROOM RATES*
Shared single: $95
Private single: $110-125
Shared double: $95
Private double: $110-$125
Each additional person: $25
Children: 6 and under free
(*Rates reflect cash price. Add 5% for credit cards.
Rates include local taxes)

This Victorian-style home is near the top of East Hill Road and boasts a beautiful view of Kachemak Bay and the Homer Spit. The two-story home has five large bedrooms. Three have private baths and two share a

bath. Two of the rooms have private balconies.

Amenities at Victorian Heights include a living room with TV, a whirl-pool bath, limited freezer space, a barbecue grill, a crib and laundry facilities on request. A self-serve continental breakfast is available before 7 a.m. From 7 a.m. to 9 a.m., the Clays serve a delightful breakfast.

"Every year, Phil and I marvel at how many wonderful people come into our lives as a result of our bed and breakfast. We love our business, and it is a pleasure to make people feel at home at Victorian Heights," Tammy says.

Victorian Heights has earned a three-diamond rating from AAA.

Kenai

Kenai is the oldest city on the Kenai Peninsula. Originally inhabited by the Dena'ina Athabaskan Indians, in 1791 Russian fur traders established a trading post, Fort St. Nicholas, here, on the bluff where now stands the Holy Assumption of the Virgin Mary Russian Orthodox Church.

The church is the heart of the Old Town District, which is also the site of Fort Kenay, established after America bought the Russian America Company properties in Alaska, in 1867. Several homesteader cabins round out the Old Town District, a national historic landmark.

Kenai is reached via the Seward and Sterling Highways from Anchorage, or by air. It and neighboring city of Soldotna make up the largest population base of the Kenai Peninsula. For this reason, it is also the shopping hub of the Peninsula. Among its attractions are:

☒ *Kenai Visitors & Cultural Center* — The pride of Kenai, supporters boast that the center houses the largest mounted bird exhibit, the largest ivory collection, and the largest Alaska video library in the state. In the summer, it holds free interpretive programs on Mondays, Wednesdays and Fridays.

☒ *Kenai Fine Arts Center* — Located in Kenai's first firehall and jail, the Fine Art Center features local exhibitions, workshops, art sales and the Kenai Pottery studio.

☒ *Challenger Learning Center* — The center is designed as an innovative, imaginative place that will get kids enthusiastic about math, science and technology. Its plans include an exploratorium exhibit area open to the public.

☒ *Fishing* — Kenai sits near the mouth of the Kenai River, renowned for its king salmon sport fishing. It also sits on the bank of Cook Inlet, which offers other opportunities for salt-water fishing.

☒ *Hiking* — The Central Kenai Peninsula offers all sorts of opportunities for hiking, from the Captain Cook State Recreation Area to the Kenai National Wildlife Refuge. The Refuge headquarters in Soldotna has maps of the major trails.

For more information contact the Kenai Visitors and Convention Bureau, 11471 Kenai Spur Highway, Kenai, AK 99611, phone (907) 283-1991, www.visitkenai.com.

The Rusty Rooster Bed & Breakfast

P. O. Box 2606
Kenai, Alaska 99611
(907) 283-3938 or 877-583-3938 toll free
E-mail: dondoo@alaska.net
Mary Elliott, Host

Months Open: Year round
Hours:
Credit Cards: None
Accommodations: 3 rooms

Children Welcome: On approval
Pets Accommodated: No
Social Drinking: Yes
Smoking: Outside

ROOM RATES
Single: $50 winter; $65 summer
Double: $65 winter; $85 summer
Each additional person: $25
Children: $10

The Rusty Rooster is located between Soldotna and Kenai on Kalifornsky Beach Road. The home is an A-frame chalet with cedar-stained siding. The interior is decorated with many antiques, and boasts a fireplace, formal dining room, as well as informal dining area. In the yard are barbecue grills and picnic tables for guest use. Moose often wander through the yard.

The bedrooms are downstairs. The *Begonia Room* has a double bed and shared bath. *The Duck Room* has three twin beds. The *Route 66 Room* has a double bed and a half bath.

Mary offers a full breakfast to her guests. Menu items may include pecan waffles, quiche, eggs benedict, muffins, fruit juice and feshly ground coffee. Special needs are honored. She will also provide other meals by arrangement.

Mary is a 61-year-old mother of four and grandmother of nine. She shares her home with one small dog.

As a convenience to her guests, Mary can arrange guided salmon fishing trips on the Kenai River, arrange charters and make bed and breakfast reservations for halibut fishing out of Homer.

Ninilchik

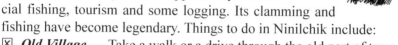

Ninilchik is a quiet village on the Sterling Highway, about halfway between Homer and Soldotna. It has its roots in both Russian and Dena'ina Athabaskan Indian traditions. One of the first colonial settlements of the Russian-America Company, the community is now supported by commercial fishing, tourism and some logging. Its clamming and fishing have become legendary. Things to do in Ninilchik include:

☒ *Old Village* — Take a walk or a drive through the old part of town, below the bridge toward the beach. Get a feel for life in the early days.

☒ *Russian Orthodox Church* — Hike up the footpath from the old village to the onion-domed church. The church, which was built in 1901, boasts one of the most spectacular settings on the entire Kenai Peninsula and has been the subject of numerous paintings and photographs.

☒ *Deep Creek* — Located just two miles south of Ninilchik, Deep Creek offers fine king salmon fishing in the early summer, and its beaches offer some of the best razor clamming to be found on the peninsula. Bring a bucket and shovel and prepare to dig, but don't forget your sport-fishing license.

☒ *Fishing Charters* — Besides offering great river fishing in the Ninilchik River and Deep Creek, Ninilchik offers great access to Cook Inlet, where anglers can try their luck at catching salmon or halibut. Several charter businesses operate out of Ninilchik.

☒ *Kenai Peninsula State Fair* — For one weekend in August the Ninilchik Fairgrounds is home to "the biggest little fair in Alaska." The fair, a popular event since 1951, attracts folks from miles around to show their garden produce, home crafts and livestock. A highlight every year is the 4H livestock show and auction. Food booths, game booths, demonstrations, ongoing entertainment, a barbecue, parade and dance add to the fun.

BLUFF HOUSE BED & BREAKFAST

P.O. Box 39327
Ninilchik, Alaska 99639
(907) 567-3605
E-mail: bluffbb@alaska.net
Web site: www.alaska.net/~bluffbb
Terry & Margie Smith, Hosts

Months Open: Year-round   **Children Welcome:** Over 16
Hours: 24   **Pets Accommodated:** No
Credit Cards: None   **Social Drinking:** Yes
Accommodations: 6 rooms   **Smoking:** No

ROOM RATES*
Single with shared bath: $75
Double with shared bath: $100
Double with private bath: $115
(*3-day minimum; king beds available for 5-day minimum stays)

Bluff House Bed & Breakfast is centrally located on the Kenai Peninsula, between the Ninilchik River and Deep Creek, overlooking Cook Inlet. Its quiet, adult atmosphere and magnificent view of three majestic volcanoes — Mount Redoubt, Mount Iliamna, and Mount Spurr Volcano — make this the perfect getaway for rest and recreation.

In the summer guests can enjoy superb freshwater and salt water fish-

ing in nearby waters, excellent razor clam digging on the beach, beachcombing, hiking, berry picking, horseback riding and wildlife viewing. Whales, seals and sea otters often can be seen offshore. Bald eagles frequently soar near the bluff. And moose can be  seen any time of the year. Other wildlife that may be seen include bear, fox, ermine, wolves, rabbits and a resident mountain goat that grazes on the bluff overlooking Deep Creek.

Winter enjoyments include snowshoeing, cross-country skiing, sledding, dog-sled rides and snowmobiling. Terry and Margie, long-time Alaskans, offer snowmobiling tours to the Caribou Hills, where there are over 200 miles of 14-foot wide, groomed trails. They have a special trip to Caribou Lake Lodge, 43 miles away, a fantastic ride that provides breathtaking panoramic views of the volcanoes across Cook Inlet, as well as Tustumena Lake, Kenai and Denali to the north and Kachemak Bay, Cape Douglas and Seldovia Point to the south. The ride to the lodge is three hours one way.

Bluff House is a two-story home, with the first floor dedicated to guests. Guests have their own living room with TV and VCR, breakfast bar with refrigerator and microwave, as well as other amenities that help make visits pleasant. The six guest rooms are spacious and complemented by modern facilities, including a Jacuzzi and sauna for your enjoyment after a fun-filled day.

Breakfast is either full-course or continental, depending on the tides, since a majority of Bluff House guests come for the area's great fishing during the summer.

"We do our best to make the Bluff House our guests' home away from home. You will arrive as guests and leave as friends. Our commitment is to share the beauty and uniqueness of our great state and to provide true Alaskan hospitality. We also refer our guests to fishing charters and are happy to make reservations for them," say Terry and Margie.

Seldovia

Seldovia is a small, picturesque community on the south side of Kachemak Bay, reachable only by boat or airplane. In the early days, Seldovia was the main community on the southern Kenai Peninsula. It was home to several canneries, and all mail and supplies destined for Homer and Anchor Point were offloaded here for transfer to those smaller communities. When the herring fishery declined, so did Seldovia's population. Today it is supported by commercial fishing and tourism. The town has old-time Alaska charm, with houses perched on rocky cliffs and boardwalks that wind along the water's edge.

Attractions include:

☒ *Fourth of July* — Seldovia residents go all out for Fourth of July, sometimes devoting an entire weekend to celebrations. So much goes on and so much fun is had that people come from as far away as Anchorage to join in the festivities. There is a parade, all sorts of games and competitions of skill — such as log rolling in Seldovia Slough — and lots of seafood to eat.

☒ *Blueberry Festival* — Some of the best blueberry picking on the Kenai Peninsula can be found here, and Seldovians annually celebrate this abundance with a day-long festival. If the thought of blueberries makes your mouth water, this one's for you.

☒ *Berry Picking* — You don't have to wait for the festival to enjoy Seldovia's largess. Starting in August, surrounding roads and trails are lined with burgeoning berry bushes. There are succulent salmonberries, in both yellow and red varieties, and blueberries so plentiful and large they look like grapes. Some of the best picking is on land belonging to the Seldovia Native Association, so check with them before you start out.

☒ *Biking and Hiking* — there are many roads and trails suitable for hiking and biking, including the road to Jakalof Bay and the Otterbahn Nature Trail that starts behind the school.

For more information, contact the Seldovia Chamber of Commerce, Drawer F, Seldovia, Alaska 99663, (907) 234-7612.

ACROSS THE BAY
TENT & BREAKFAST
ADVENTURE COMPANY

Summer
P.O. Box 81
Seldovia, AK 99663-0081
Fax: (907) 235-3633
Winter
P.O. Box 112054
Anchorage, AK 99511-2054
(907) 345-2571
Tony & Mary Jane Lastufka, Hosts

Months Open: May-September
Hours: 24
Credit Cards: VISA, MC
Accommodations: 5 canvas cabins

Children Welcome: Yes
Pets Accommodated: No
Social Drinking: Yes
Smoking: Outside only

ROOM RATES*
Tent and breakfast: $58 per person
Tent and all meals: $85 per person
(*Group rates available)

Located across Kachemak Bay from Homer and $8^1/2$ miles east of Seldovia at Kasitsna Bay, Across the Bay Tent & Breakfast Adventure Company offers visitors a unique Alaskan experience. Hosts Tony and Mary Jane Lastufka built their summer home on Kasitsna Bay in 1978, and now use it as the base for their tent and breakfast operation.

Accommodations consist of five wall tents, that sleep from two to five people, or a maximum of 15 guests at a time. The tents sit on wooden platforms and are rain and insect proof, and they are carpeted. They come equipped with beds, mattresses and pillows. Guests must bring their own sleeping bags, but wool blankets are provided. Hot showers and a sauna are available. Sanitary facilities are "two of the prettiest outhouses in Alaska."

Nestled in the woods, or overlooking the bay, each tent site has its own special character and is both comfortable and in harmony with the wilderness surroundings.

Breakfast consists of homemade granola, fresh muffins, fruit, fresh-ground coffee and tea. Lunch and dinner are available for an extra fee and may include halibut, grilled salmon, oysters, homemade caviar and salads made with home-grown greens.

Guests can choose from a variety of activities, including tide pool exploration, hiking, fishing, beachcombing or mountain biking. Bring your own bike or rent one for $15 a half day or $25 a full day. Your hosts can suggest trails to take or can arrange a guided trip. Guided kayak tours are available for $95 per person per day.

KASITSNA BAY GRANOLA

1/2 c. olive oil	1/2 c. wheat germ
1/2 c. honey	1 c. raisins
1/2 tsp. salt	1 c. diced dried papaya
1 T. vanilla	1 c. whole cashews
8 c. old-fashioned rolled oats	1 c. whole almonds
1/2 c. sesame seeds	1/2 c. sunflower seeds

Heat oil, honey, salt & vanilla in 375° oven until thin. Add oats and blend; bake, stirring every 5-8 minutes, until brown. Add remaining ingredients, mix and allow to cool. Serves 15.

SELDOVIA ROWING CLUB
BED & BREAKFAST

P. O. Box 41
Seldovia, Alaska 99663
(907) 234-7614
E-mail: rowing@ptialaska.net
Web site: www.ptialaska.net/~rowing
Susan Mumma, Host

Months Open: All year
Hours: Check-in 1:30 p.m.; out, noon
Credit Cards: VISA, MC
Accommodations: 2 suites

Children Welcome: Yes
Pets Accommodated: No
Social Drinking: Yes
Smoking: On deck only

ROOM RATES
Single: $60 winter; $85 summer
Double: $85 winter; $125 summer
Each additional person: $25
Children: $25

Seldovia Rowing Club is located on the historic old Boardwalk on

the Seldovia Slough. It is convenient to downtown, only a block from the harbor and one-half mile from the airport. The house has a traditional Old Seldovia exterior and is built on pilings above the water, where the tide is always changing. Inside, the house is appointed with Victorian antiques and nautical paraphernalia.

The three-story house has a fireplace, two decks, two living rooms, and private baths in both suites. Guest accommo-

dations are on the first two floors. Susan's studio and gallery are on the third floor.

Each suite has a living room, private deck, private bath and queen beds in the bedroom. The kitchen area is downstairs. Guests can fish for king salmon off the decks, best in May and June.

Breakfast at the Rowing Club is gourmet and served by candle light, ensuite, at your own elegant table, at the time of your choice. The menu includes choice of omelettes, "Slumgullion," French toast, crepes, pancakes, or "host's choice." Breakfast is served with healthy potatoes, muffins and juice. Coffee, tea and cocoa are available at all times.

Susan is a practicing artist, who can be found most days painting watercolors in her upstairs gallery, which she shares with her three cats: Garlic, Boogie and Sawyer. She also collects and sells early American pressed glass at her shop, "A Touch of Glass." An avid sailor, she has her own fleet of small wooden boats.

Susan offers car service between the Rowing Club and the harbor or airport. She can also arrange a travel package for guests.

Guests at the Rowing Club can enjoy hiking, fishing, kayaking, wildlife viewing, shopping, or just relaxing in quiet, peaceful serenity, enjoying the scenery, napping or sunbathing.

SLUMGULLION

1 or 2 potatoes, steamed
Some broccoli, carrots, onion, multi-colored peppers
and other available vegetables, steamed
eggs, cheese and Seldovia Rowing Club secret spice

Mix them all together in a pan and fry lightly in butter. Serve with Special Seldovia Rowing Club Muffins and Juice, and *Voila!*...the perfect breakfast!

SWAN HOUSE SOUTH B&B SELDOVIA

Mailing Address:
6840 Crooked Tree Drive
Anchorage, Alaska 99516
Summer: (907) 234-8888
Year round: (907) 346-3033; (800) 921-1900
Fax: (907) 234-8887
E-mail: swan1@alaska.net
Web page: www.alaskaswanhouse.com
Judy and Jerry Swanson, Hosts

Months Open: Mid-May to mid-Sept.
Credit Cards: Major cards accepted
Social Drinking: Yes
Accommodations: 4 luxury suites, private guest cottage

Hours: 8 a.m. - 10 p.m.
Children/pets welcome: Inquire
Smoking: No

ROOM RATES
$129-$249
Each additional
person: $49

"Seldovia's finest! New, comfortable, clean, modern rooms, with a view from every room," says host Judy Swanson.

Located a short five-minute walk from downtown Seldovia, the 3,500-square-foot Swan House South combines convenience with a peaceful, relaxing, smoke-free environment for the perfect adult getaway.

It has its own private dock, and the closest salmon-fishing hole is just a two-minute walk away. The airport is a mere 10-minute walk. The guest rooms were recently converted into suites, each with its own private bath and sitting room with VCR. The *Tree House Suite* has a private balcony with a waterfront view and is a favorite for honeymooners. This room has a tub and shower. The *Garden Suite* faces Graduation Peak and is the only room with a king-size log bed. Relax on the comfy sofa with a good book, or watch a movie in the sunken sitting room. The *Eagle's Nest Suite* has a wonderful waterfront view from the sitting room, while the bedroom overlooks the mountains. The *Tidewater Suite,* on the main level, is also a waterfront-view room (the largest suite) and can sleep four. It has a large bathroom with tub and shower. This suite has its own deck entrance to view the gorgeous sunsets. For special occasions, try the new waterfront guest cottage, *The Boathouse,* that sits directly above the water. You can view the salmon, sea otters and eagles up close from this private retreat on the 50-foot dock. Suites and guesthouse rates include two free mountain bike rentals.

A full breakfast is offered with the suite rates; the *Boathouse* rates include a continental breakfast for your privacy. In the main house, you can expect breakfast to be either almond croissant French toast, sourdough blueberry pancakes, Belgian waffles with homemade syrups, or eggs with reindeer sausage, along with Judy's famous fruit smoothie. Fresh ground coffee and teas are always available.

POWER DRINK

1 c. plain yogurt	2 T. wheat germ
1 banana	2 T. honey
2 c. frozen fruit (any)	1 c. juice (any)
1 c. fresh fruit (any)	

Mix all ingredients together in a blender. This drink comes out different each time you make it. The first two ingredients are the basis for the drink. Blueberries will turn it purple, mangos will keep it on the yellow/orange side. Top with whipped cream and a fresh mint leaf. Serves 8.

Seward

Seward is the southern terminus of the Alaska Railroad and is one of the few planned cities in Alaska. Like many Alaskan towns, it has had its share of booms and busts, from its heyday during railroad construction years to its near destruction during the 1964 Alaska earthquake. Today it is enjoying prosperity from its many commercial activities, most of which are centered on the sea, and tourism. It is a popular port of call for many cruise ships during the summer and a mecca for silver-salmon fishermen. The Alaska State Ferry *Tustumena* offers a weekly connection to Homer. Community highlights include:

☒ **Kenai Fjords National Park** — A 669,000-acre park which takes in Harding Icefield, a remnant of the ice age which holds some of the most rugged terrain in Alaska, and miles and miles of spectacular coastline. Several commercial operations offer half-day or day-long wildlife- and glacier-viewing trips by boat along the coastline. Park headquarters is near the harbor.

☒ **Exit Glacier** — Only a few miles from downtown Seward, the glacier is part of Harding Icefield. Park rangers lead walks in the summer. It's a short, easy hike from the parking area to the base of the glacier. On sunny days, the blue of the ice is spectacular.

☒ **Mount Marathon Run** — Held on the Fourth of July each year, this grueling race to the top of the 3,022-foot mountain and back attracts hundreds of runners and spectators annually. It's the key event in Seward's July 4 celebrations.

☒ **Seward Silver Salmon Derby** — This week-long fishing derby takes place in August and offers a prize of $10,000 for the largest silver salmon caught.

☒ **Seward Marine Center** — A branch of the University of Alaska, the center offers films, tours of the facility and displays of marine life.

☒ **Alaska SeaLife Center** — Built with money from the *Exxon Valdez* oil spill settlement, the SeaLife Center is a research facility which also houses an aquarium, seabird aquarium, and other marine life displays.

☒ **Chugach Heritage Center** — This newest of museums focuses on the cultural heritage of Alaska Natives of the Southcentral coastal area. The short play about native traditions is a must-see.

For more information, contact the Seward Chamber of Commerce at 2001 Seward Highway, Seward, AK 99664, (907) 224-8051, fax (907) 224-5353.

BELL-IN-THE-WOODS B&B

P. O. Box 345
Seward, Alaska 99664
(907) 224-7271; Fax (907) 224-7271
E-mail: bellwoodbnb@juno.com
Web site: www.bellinthewoodbnb.com
Jerry and Peggy Woods, Hosts

Months Open: Year round
Hours: Check-in 5-7 p.m.; out, 10 a.m.
Credit Cards: MC, VISA, DS
Accommodations: 5 rooms, 2 suites

Children Welcome: Yes
Pets Accommodated: No
Social Drinking: Yes
Smoking: No

ROOM RATES
Single: $50-$100 winter; $99-$170 summer
Double: $50-$100 winter; $99-$170 summer
Each additional person: $25
Children: $25

Bell-in-the-Woods B&B is a 5,200-square-foot home built to serve as a bed and breakfast. The two-story house is located in a wooded setting, with easy Seward Highway access, just six miles from Seward. The guest common area has cable TV, VCR, fireplace, library and telephone. Laundry facilities are available, and there is a large deck where guests can enjoy spectacular mountain views. The house is decorated in farm-country style, with some antiques.

All guest rooms have private baths, and the two suites have kitchenettes as well. The *Salmonberry* and *Blueberry* rooms are furnished with twin beds, which can be converted to a king-size bed. The *Cranberry* and

Mossberry Rooms have a queen bed, and the *Raspberry Room* a king bed. All have comforters and a minimum of two pillows per bed. One of the baths has a jacuzzi tub and shower. The *Salmonberry Room* is handicapped-accessible and has an attached bath that complies with ADA requirements. The two suites have a bedroom, daybed area, kitchen area and dining area, as well as private baths.

Breakfast at Bell-in-the-Woods is full and hearty. It may include baked bacon-wrapped eggs, skillet fried potatoes with light Hollandaise sauce, fresh fruit, orange juice, wheat bread toast or homemade sweet bread, coffee and tea. Afternoon or early evening coffee and cookies are also available.

Jerry Woods is a retired electrical engineer. Peggy manages the local dental office and assists in hosting the B&B.

A one-night deposit is required to hold your reservation and 7 days' notice is requried for cancellations.

THE FARM
BED & BREAKFAST INN

P.O. Box 305
Seward, Alaska 99664
(907) 224-5691; Fax (907) 224-5698
Jack & Joanne Hoogland and Carol Thomassen, Hosts

Months Open: Year-round
Hours: 24
Credit Cards: MC, VISA, DS, AMEX
Accommodations: 15 rooms

Children Welcome: Yes
Pets Accommodated: Inquire
Social Drinking: Yes
Smoking: On patios & in yard

ROOM RATES*
Summer: $65-$100
Winter: $45-$75
(*Rates given for single or double)
Each additional person: $15
Children 5 and under free

Located just three miles north of Seward on Salmon Creek Road, The Farm is a remodeled farmhouse on 10 acres. It offers guests private decks and patios, a hammock, lawn chairs, barbecue and picnic table, and walking in the surrounding grassy field.

Accommodations range from economy-priced bungalow units to luxurious kitchenette units. There is a cable TV and telephone in every room. The bungalow has one large room with a private bath and two smaller rooms that share a bath. There are four sleeping cottages, with either a queen-size bed or two twin beds and private baths. In the main house, the *King Room* has a king-size, canopied bed and a twin bed, as well as a private bath; the *Queen Room* is large enough for four people, and comes with queen-size bed and twin bed and its own private deck. It shares a bath with *Jack's Room*, which has a private entrance and deck, beautiful view and queen-size bed. The *E-Z Room* is on the first floor near the dining area and laundry facilities and offers easy access. It has a queen-size bed and twin bed and has a private bath.

The four kitchenette units offer luxurious and spacious kitchens, complete with refrigerator/freezer, range, microwave, coffee pot and utensils. They are available wth queen-size and two twin beds, queen-size and twin bed, or three twin beds, and have private phone lines.

The continental-style breakfast features more than 20 types of cereal, as well as bananas, three types of bread for toast, bagels and cream cheese, fresh-ground coffee, tea, orange juice, milk, hot chocolate, and half and half.

Jack, a retired longshoreman, moved to Alaska in 1944. Joanne and Carol are both life-long Alaskans. Joanne taught at the Seward High School for 31 years, until she retired. Carol is the mother of two young Alaskans and spends her summers helping her parents run The Farm. Golden retriever "Huki" helps to welcome guests.

MIDDLETON ISLAND TURKEY

1.5 lbs. halibut fillets	1 c. shredded cheese
1 box StoveTop stuffing	1 can Campbell's mushroom
(your favorite flavor)	soup
Croutons	

Rinse and pat dry halibut fillets. Prepare stuffing mix per directions on box. If halibut is very moist, decrease water in stuffing preparation accordingly. In a 1-1/2 to 2 qt. casserole dish, coated with Pam, layer ingredients as follows: halibut, stuffing, halibut, stuffing, halibut, mushroom soup, cheese. Bake, covered, in a 350° oven for 45 minutes. Remove lid, sprinkle top with croutons and place back in oven, uncovered, for 10 more minutes.

Soldotna

Soldotna straddles the Sterling Highway, 148 miles from Anchorage. The Kenai River runs through town, attracting thousands of hopeful anglers every year. Begun in the early 1940s as an agricultural community, it soon found itself the center of oil exploration and activity. The nearby Swanson River oil field was the first big oil discovery and drilling effort in Alaska, followed by finds in Cook Inlet. It is now the seat of borough government and, with its sister city Kenai, 10 miles to the north, is the major population center for the Kenai Peninsula. Among the things to do and see locally are:

⊠ *Central Peninsula Sports Center* — Located on Kalifornski Beach Road near downtown Soldotna, the center offers a variety of recreational opportunities and special events throughout the year.

⊠ *Soldotna Progress Days* — This annual celebration takes place in late July and features parades, special dinners, arts and crafts booths, car races and a car show, as well as other fun events.

⊠ *Rodeo Days* — Riders from all over the Kenai Peninsula compete in rodeos at the Soldotna Arena every summer, including the big rodeo during Soldotna Progress Days. On "off" weekends, there are a variety of shows and workshops to view.

⊠ *Museums* — There is a small museum featuring artifacts from Soldotna's past located near Centennial Park, next to the visitor center in Soldotna. A short drive away, in Kenai, Fort Kenay and the Kenai Historical Museum offer a look at the area's Russian and Native heritage. Next to Fort Kenay is the Russian Orthodox Church, which was built in 1896 and is the oldest standing Russian Orthodox Church in Alaska.

⊠ *Hiking, Skiing* — There are a variety of trails to hike in the Kenai National Moose Range. Check at the range's visitor center for maps. In the winter, many of these trails are open to cross-country skiers, along with a trail system behind Skyview High School.

For more information, contact the Soldotna Chamber of Commerce, Box 236, Soldotna, AK 99669; (907) 262-1337.

BLAZY'S BED & BREAKFAST

P.O. Box 758
Soldotna, Alaska 99669
(907) 262-4591; Fax (907) 262-4934
E-mail: mayor@gci.net
Ken & Mavis Lancaster, Hosts

Months Open: Year-round
Hours: 24
Credit Cards: None
Accommodations: 2 suites

Children Welcome: Yes
Pets Accommodated: Inquire
Social Drinking: Yes
Smoking: Outside only

ROOM RATES
Single: $70
Double: $80
Each additional person: $10
Children: $10

Blazy Bed and Breakfast is within walking distance of the world-famous Kenai River and downtown Soldotna. The grounds are pleasant, and the house includes a large deck with a barbecue available for guest use. Hosts Ken and Mavis will arrange fishing charters for guests, if desired.

Each of the large suites features queen-size beds, and has its own bathroom, kitchenette, color TV and phone.

Continental breakfasts include fresh fruit, toast, cereal, muffins, cinnamon rolls, juice, tea and coffee.

Ken was born in Alaska and serves as Soldotna's mayor. Mavis is a

transplant from Australia. They share their home with two shihtzu dogs.

"Join us and experience real Alaskan living in our home. Enjoy a leisurely stroll to the best fishing in the world, or just relax on the back deck and enjoy the surroundings," Mavis says.

CAPTAIN BLIGH'S BEAVER CREEK
LODGE AND GUIDE SERVICES

P.O. Box 4300
Soldotna, Alaska 99669
(907) 283-7550 summer; (907) 262-7919 winter
E-mail: bligh@ptialaska.net
Web page: www.ptialaska.net/~bligh
Clinton & Dolores (Dodie) Coligan, Hosts

Months Open: May 15 - Oct. 1
Hours: 24
Credit Cards: None
Accommodations: 5 rooms, 2 cabins

Children Welcome: All ages
Pets Accommodated: Yes
Social Drinking: Yes
Smoking: In lodge

CABIN & ROOM RATES
Double: $90-$130
Each additional person: Varies

Set on the banks of the world-renowned Kenai River, Beaver Creek Lodge is located four miles upstream from Cook Inlet and three miles from downtown Kenai. Situated in a serene and uniquely Alaskan setting, with a breathtaking view of the surrounding mountains and river, this lodge is totally private.

The Main Lodge

Beaver Creek Lodge consists of four separate facilities: the main lodge, which has two large bedrooms and houses up to eight guests, three adjacent self-contained units which can house up to eight people each, and three large two-bedroom log homes. The homes are completely furnished with every amenity, including washer and dryer,

Two-bedroom log home

and are ideal for two couples vacationing together or a family. All units are tastefully decorated with artwork, trophies and fish mounts. Each has a private bath.

Breakfast in the main lodge is continental. Guests in self-contained units and cabins do their own cooking.

Beaver Creek Lodge is a full-service lodge which, aside from picturesque, comfortable accommodations, offers guided angling for all species of fish in the river or nearby Inlet, fly-outs to remote lakes and rivers, bear watching, and fly-

fishing for trophy rainbow trout. Most visitors select a package, Clint Coligan says. "However, we welcome all calls for either fishing or lodging on a daily basis as well."

87¹/₂ lb. King Salmon

Clint and Dodie have been Alaska residents for 40 years and have been welcoming guests to their lodge since 1975. "We are committed to offering true Alaskan hospitality to every guest during their stay with us," Clint says.

Very happy angler

POSEY'S KENAI RIVER HIDEAWAY BED & BREAKFAST

34025 Keystone Dr.
Soldotna, Alaska 99669
(907) 262-7430; Fax (907) 262-7430
June Posey, Host

Months Open: Year-round
Hours: 4 a.m. - 10 p.m.
Credit Cards: MC, VISA
Accommodations: 10 rooms

Children Welcome: Over 11
Pets Accommodated: No
Social Drinking: Yes
Smoking: Yes

ROOM RATES
Per person: $75 summer, $60 winter

June Posey's Kenai River Hideaway is a huge, cedar-sided "four-plex turned bed and breakfast" on the banks of the Kenai River. It is conveniently located just 15 minutes from the Soldotna airport and 30 minutes form the Kenai airport.

The house has two three-bedroom suites and two two-bedroom suites, for a total of ten guest bedrooms, two of which have private baths. June describes her rooms as "nicely furnished, contemporary." Each suite has a refrigerator with ice maker. The beautiful *Honeymoon Suite* comes complete with its own private bath, shower, Jacuzzi and king-size bed.

June has received five-star ratings from guests for the meals she serves. Breakfast consists of coffee and juice, fruit, eggs, bacon, waffles or pancakes with June's own pecan maple butter. There are barbecue grills and picnic tables in the yard for those who want to barbecue steaks or the salmon they've caught fresh just that morning.

June can arrange guided salmon fishing trips on the Kenai River, known for excellent fishing for sockeye and silver salmon, Dolly Varden and rainbow trout. She will also be glad to arrange charters and make bed-and-breakfast reservations out of Homer for halibut fishing.

WOODY BIRD CIRCLE B&B

P. O Box 4353
Soldotna, Alaska 99669
(907) 262-9031 or 877-860-9031 toll free; Fax (907) 260-7598
E-mail: woodybrd@alaska.net
Web site: www.woodybird.com
Linda Story, Host

Months Open: Year round
Hours: Check-in after 3; out 11 a.m.
Credit Cards: VISA, MC
Accommodations: 3 rooms

Children Welcome: Inquire
Pets Accommodated: No
Social Drinking: Yes
Smoking: Outside

ROOM RATES
Summer: $75-$95
Winter: $50

Woody Bird Circle B&B is a comfortable, wood-sided home located just three miles from the Kenai River and downtown Soldotna. It is convenient to the Swanson River Canoe Trail system and to many hiking trails. The house is comfortably furnished and decorated with Alaska prints, photos and artifacts. The yard is landscaped with Alaska wildflowers.

There are three guest rooms at Woody Bird. The *Birch Room* is furnished with an antique oak bed and dresser. It shares a bath with the *Willow*

Room, which has twin beds and a private entrance onto the deck. The *Spruce Room* has a queen-size brass bed and private bath. All rooms are decorated with Alaska pictures.

Homemade muffins, banana bread, and the like, are left out for early morning adventurers. Guests who have time for a more leisurely breakfast are served a full meal consisting of such delicacies as apple oven pancake, blueberry pancakes, farmers casserole, fresh fruit, sausage and fresh orange juice. Packed lunches are available at extra cost and snacks are offered to fit the occasion.

Linda Story came to Alaska as a tourist and stayed. She is a novice birder and also enjoys hiking, canoeing, wildflower identification, berry picking and mushrooming. She shares her quarters with a blue-crowned Conure parrot.

"Woody Bird Circle is a great home base for birding, hiking, golfing, fishing, clamming, beachcombing, flightseeing, rafting and an array of Alaskan adventures," Linda says.

APPLE OVEN PANCAKE

3 eggs	1/2 c. flour
1/2 c. milk	2 apples
2 tsp. cinnamon	1/4 c. sugar/brown sugar or honey
6 T. butter	

Slice apples and saute them in butter; add sugar and cinnamon. In separate bowl, beat eggs, add milk and then flour. Put apple mixture in bottom of baking dish; pour milk, egg and flour mixture over apples and bake at 400° for 25 minutes. Serve with vanilla yogurt or whipped cream.

Recipe is just right for two individual oven dishes or can be doubled to fit larger needs.

Kodiak

Located about 45 air miles from Anchorage, in the Gulf of Alaska, Kodiak Island is home to one of the largest commercial fishing ports in the United States. It is also the site of the earliest European settlement in Alaska and, at 100 miles long, is the largest island in Alaska. The largest community on the island also bears its name, Kodiak. From this port each year, hundreds of boats sail to fish for salmon, shrimp, herring, halibut, crab and other seafood. After the earliest Russian settlement at Three Saints Bay on the eastern end of the island was destroyed by a tidal wave in the late 1700s, the center of Russian-America company activities was moved to Kodiak.

Attractions for visitors include:

☒ **The Baranof Museum** — Also known as the Erskine House, the museum was built in 1808 as a warehouse for sea otter pelts, and now houses exhibits of Russian and Native cultures.

☒ **Russian Orthodox Church** — The parish and church were established in 1794, but the church itself has been rebuilt three times after being destroyed by fire. The current structure was built in 1954 and houses paintings and icons dating back to the czarist period in Russia.

☒ **Kodiak Crab Festival** — This week-long celebration features parades, carnival booths, skill competitions, a queen contest, and boat, kayak and foot races.

☒ **Alutiiq Museum** — This thematic museum, Kodiak's newest, focuses on the history and culture of the Alutiiq people of Kodiak and Alaska's Southcentral Gulf Coast. The Alutiiq were living, hunting and fishing in this area for centuries before the Russians even glimpsed the island, and their knowledge and generosity made it possible for the Russians to survive.

☒ **Kodiak Island National Wildlife Refuge** — Established in 1941 to preserve the natural habitat of Kodiak bears and other wildlife, the refuge encompasses nearly 2,500 square miles on Kodiak and Afognak Islands. Activities include fishing, photography, camping, canoeing, and backpacking. For more information, call the refuge manager's office at (907) 478-2600.

EMERALD ISLE
BED & BREAKFAST

1214 Madsen
P.O. Box 3567
Kodiak, Alaska 99615
(907) 486-4893 or (866) 486-4892; Fax (907) 486-8120
E-mail: luanne@kodiaklodging.com
Web site: www.kodiaklodging.com
Luanne & Al Cottle, Hosts

Months Open: Year-round
Hours: 7 a.m. - 11 p.m.
Credit Cards: VISA, MC
Accommodations: 3 rooms

Children Welcome: Yes
Pets Accommodated: No
Social Drinking: Yes
Smoking: No

ROOM RATES*
$85 single, $95 double
*Limit of 2 per room at quoted rates

Emerald Isle Bed & Breakfast is a two-story home located a leisurely 20-minute walk from downtown Kodiak. Your hosts live upstairs with their toy poodle, Ginger, and cat, Muffin. One bedroom with private bath is upstairs. The guests in this room share the common area with guests downstairs. The downstairs is devoted to guests and includes its own living room, decorated with Alaska art, a large Alaska library, dining room, laundry

room, and two bedrooms with private baths. Rooms have king-size and queen-size beds. There's a microwave oven, small refrigerator, freezer, coffee pot, hot-water pot, TV, private entrance, and barbecue on the deck.

Breakfast is hearty and includes cereals, milk, juice, Denver omelets, breakfast casseroles, fresh baked muffins, sweet rolls or bread, and coffee, hot chocolate and tea. Popcorn, Hershey's Kisses, and a variety of hot chocolate flavors, teas and coffee are available at any time.

Al and Luanne are long-time Alaskans, Luanne coming to Alaska in 1949 and Al arriving in the 1950s. The two have traveled extensively throughout the state and have lived in Petersburg, Wrangell, Juneau, Douglas, Fairbanks, Fort Yukon, Ketchikan and Kodiak. They welcome guests and want them to feel that Emerald Isle Bed & Breakfast is their home away from home.

SALMONBERRY PIE

2 cups salmonberries   1 c. sugar
baked pie shell   2 T. cornstarch
1 c. water   4 T. raspberry jello
4 oz. cream cheese

Spread cream cheese over cooled pie crust. place berries over cream cheese. In a saucepan, mix water, sugar and cornstarch and cook, stirring, until thick and clear. Add jello. Pour over salmonberries in shell and chill. Top with whipped cream.

Matanuska-Susitna Valley

The Matanuska-Susitna Valley is both bedroom and playground for Anchorage, as well as the gateway to Anchorage, Interior Alaska, and to the splendor of Denali National Park. American settlement of the area stems from the Gold Rush days, when prospectors flooded all over Alaska seeking gold. Settlers soon followed, starting farms to feed Alaska's growing population. Further settlement was encouraged by the building of the Alaska Railroad, from Seward to Fairbanks, and by the establishment of an agricultural colony at Palmer during the Great Depression. Its proximity to the state's most populous city ensured its continued growth, and in the 1970s Alaskans voted to move the state capital from Juneau to the more centrally located valley community of Willow. Later they decided not to fund the move, so it never came about, much to the relief of Juneau folks and some valley residents as well.

The valley is blessed by an abundance of fish-rich lakes, rivers and streams. It is rimmed by magnificent mountains and is loomed over by America's largest mountain, spectacular Mount McKinley, on the northwest. Its warm, generally sunny summers and cold winters attract hundreds of recreationalists year-round.

Hiking, boating, fishing, camping, climbing, cross-country skiing, snowmachining and dog-sledding are some of the many outdoor activities that can be enjoyed here. A highlight of the summer is the Alaska State Fair in Palmer, a two-week event that draws thousands of visitors to the valley every year.

Palmer

Palmer was established in 1935 as the destination for farmers who came to colonize the Matanuska Valley under the U.S. government's New Deal program. Today, Palmer is one of the few towns in Alaska whose residents rely on agriculture for their living. Some of the largest vegetables grown in Alaska are produced here, and they can be seen at the annual Alaska State Fair, held at the end of August.

It is the seat of Matanuska-Susitna Borough government and the site of the valley's hospital. Among its attractions are:

☒ *Colony Christmas* — Highlights of this annual event, held the second weekend in December, include the lighting of the community Christmas tree, reindeer sled rides, horsedrawn wagon or sleigh rides, an arts and crafts fair, contests and fireworks.

☒ *Colony Days* — Held the third weekend in June, this festival celebrates the people who came to the valley in 1935. Events include a parade, shopping-cart race, arts and crafts fair, children's games and contests, 5k and 10k races and a street dance.

☒ *Independence Mine State Historic Park* — Relics from the early mining era are displayed at the visitor center and some of the early facilities have been restored as part of the park. This is a popular cross-country skiing area in the winter, and a private lodge maintains a system of trails for the purpose. Hiking and berry picking are good summer activities.

☒ *Matanuska Glacier* — Although the glacier has been receding in recent years, it remains one of Alaska's most accessible and spectacular glaciers. You can drive right up to this magnificent river of ice or view it from the highway.

☒ *Musk Ox Farm* — Guided tours of the world's only domestic musk ox farm are available daily from May through September. Admission is charged.

☒ *Palmer Visitor Center* — Located in the heart of town, the visitor center offers information about area activities. Adjoining the center is the "Agricultural Showcase" garden.

For more information, contact the Palmer Chamber of Commerce, P. O. Box 45, Palmer, AK 99645, (907) 745-2880, fax (907) 746-4164.

COLONY INN

P.O. Box 118
Palmer, Alaska 99645
(907) 745-3330; Fax (907) 745-3330
Intra-Alaska: 1-800-478-ROOM
Janet Kincaid, Host

Months Open: Year round
Hours: 24, register at Valley Hotel
Credit Cards: VISA, MC, AMEX, DS
Accommodations: 12 rooms

Children Welcome: Yes
Pets Accommodated: No
Social Drinking: No
Smoking: No

ROOM RATES
$85, all year, double or single
Each additional person: $5

Staying at the Colony Inn is like stepping back into the pages of history. The Inn began its existence in 1935, when it was constructed as the Teacher's Dormitory for the Matanuska Valley Colony. The colony, part of President Franklin D. Roosevelt's New Deal Program, brought over 200 families from the drought-stricken American Midwest to establish a farming community in Palmer.

The Inn is located behind the Visitor's Center, across the street from the Colony House Museum, right in the middle of the Matanuska Colony Historic District. The building itself is three stories and full of antiques.

There are 12 rooms at the Inn, each with its own bath. Ten rooms have a whirlpool tub; the remaining two have showers only. Each room has a telephone, TV, and quilts on the beds. There is a fireplace in the great room, lots of books to read, and free laundry facilities.

Rates include a $2 per person breakfast voucher, based on double occupancy. Breakfast is available at the Inn Cafe, which is located at the nearby Valley Hotel. The cafe is also open for dinner Friday and Saturday evenings.

Host Janet Kincaid is an Alaska pioneer, having lived here since 1954. She has six children and 19 grandchildren, all living in the Matanuska Valley. She is also a former borough assemblywoman and is active in the local Lions Club, Chamber of Commerce and Salvation Army.

HATCHER PASS BED & BREAKFAST

HC 05 Box 6797-D
Palmer, AK 99645
(907) 745-6788; Fax (907) 745-6787
E-mail: cabins@hatcherpassbb.com
Web page: www.hatcherpassbb.com
Dan & Liz Hejl, Hosts

Months open: Year round	**Children welcome:** Yes
Hours: 9 a.m.-9 p.m.	**Pets accommodated:** Yes
Credit cards: VISA, MC	**Social drinking:** Yes
Accommodations: 3 cabins	**Smoking:** Outside

ROOM RATES*
Single: $70 summer; $60 winter
Double: $80 summer, $70 winter
Each additional person: $10
Children: $10
Ask about our weekly rates
(*Please add 5% sales tax)

Hatcher Pass Bed & Breakfast is located 50 miles north of Anchorage at Mile 6.6 Palmer Fishhook Road or Mile 10 of the Wasilla Fishhook Road. At the base of Hatcher Pass, it is 10 miles from Independence Mine. The

Palmer Fish Hook Road intersects the Glenn Highway two miles north of downtown Palmer. The Wasilla Fish Hook Road intersects the George Parks Highway in Wasilla, where it starts out as Main Street.

There are three log cabins, separated from the main house and from each other to ensure guests' privacy. Each cabin is warmly decorated to provide a cozy, comfortable and uniquely Alaskan stay. Each cabin is heated with natural gas and is fully equipped with electricity. Each also has a private bath and a small kitchenette, furnished with dishes, cooktop stove, tea pot, coffee pot and refrigerator. Sleeping accommodations vary from cabin to cabin, with queen-size, double, and bunk beds being available.

For breakfast, the cabins are stocked with cold cereal, milk, juice and a variety of hot beverages, sausage, eggs, and muffins/bread for you to enjoy at your convenience.

"We offer you the best in authentic Alaska living to make your stay more comfortable," say hosts Dan and Liz Hejl. They and their two children are life-long Alaskans. Dan is an avid hunter and fisherman with a wealth of information to share in his area. Son Josh is an outdoor enthusiast in many areas, including skiing, biking, rock climbing, camping and hiking. "We love Alaska and hope all visitors will enjoy their stay in the Great State."

Talkeetna

Talkeetna is known the world round as the jump-off place for climbing expeditions to Mount McKinley. Each year hundreds of climbers embark from the Talkeetna airport enroute to the Kahiltna Glacier or other starting point for the grueling climb. McKinley, or Denali as the locals call it, is known as the weather maker, and many hopeful climbers never make it all the way to the top because of severe weather conditions.

But the community attracts more than just climbers. Many southcentral Alaska residents enjoy the 111-mile drive up the George Parks Highway to Talkeetna because it offers unparalleled views of the mountain. And at the end of the road is a community of friendly, fun-loving folks. Attractions include:

☒ *Miner's Day* — Held the weekend before Memorial Day, this annual celebration features a turkey shoot, art and craft fair, street dance, and action-packed outhouse race.

☒ *Moose Dropping Festival* — This annual excuse for a party is a fundraiser for the Talkeetna museum. Highlights include a parade, food and game booths, moose-dropping throwing contest and other adventurous events. It's held the second Saturday in July.

☒ *Talkeetna Museum* — The museum, which is housed in a schoolhouse built in 1936, displays historical artifacts and items relating to local mountain-climbing history. A walking-tour map of Talkeetna's historical sites is available.

DENALI VIEW BED & BREAKFAST

HC 89, Box 8360
Talkeetna, Alaska 99676
(907) 733-2778; Fax (907) 733-2778
E-mail: info@denaliview.com
Web sites: www.denaliview.com
www.alaskaone.com/denviewraft
LesLee and Norm Solberg, Hosts

Months Open: March-October
Hours: 6 a.m. - midnight
check-in after 5 p.m.
Credit Cards: MC, VISA
Accommodations: 2 rooms, 1 cabin

Children Welcome: Inquire
Pets Accommodated: Inquire
Social Drinking: Yes
Smoking: Outside,
in designated areas

ROOM RATES
Single: $85
Double: $100
Cabin: $110
Each additional person: $50
(Plus 5% bed tax)

Denali View Bed & Breakfast is a cozy country home with a hunting and fishing motif. It is located 12 miles south of Talkeetna and overlooks the upper Susitna Valley, with a spectacular view of Denali (Mt. McKinley) and the Alaska and Talkeetna Ranges.

Denali View has two rooms, both with antique and iron queen-size

beds and TVs. Small groups can be accommodated by using the den. All rooms have private baths and queen-size beds. The cabin sleeps three.

The morning's fare is a full breakfast of home-cooked specialties, fresh fruit, homemade bread, coffee and juice. It is served between 7 a.m. and 9 a.m. unless otherwise arranged.

Denali View and the Talkeetna area have lots to offer visitors: views of 20,320-foot Denali, mountain climbing, hiking, biking, river rafting the three local rivers, hunting, skiing, dog sledding, snowmachining, lake and river fishing, bird-watching, flightseeing, photography, shopping in Talkeetna, or just relaxing on the deck.

Norm was a teacher and coach for 28 years, a hunter all his life, and a fishing guide for 20 years. Now he is oarsman for Denali View's river rafting business. LesLee has extensive experience in hospitality and is a great tour guide. Bonnie, LesLee's mom, says she comes to Denali View in summer to "help the guests fall in love with Alaska as I have."

DENALI VIEW'S EGG SOUFFLE

5 eggs, beaten 'til frothy
1 T. salsa sauce
$^1/_3$ c. shredded cheddar cheese

About $^1/_2$ c. buttermilk
1 T. Bisquick

Spray two oven-proof berry bowls, small cereal bowls, or coffee cups with Pam or similar spray. Mix all ingredients together. Pour into bowls and bake for 45 minutes at 350° or until done and golden. Run a knife around the edges to release and carefully slide out onto plate.

Wasilla

Wasilla, located on the George Parks Highway 42 miles north of Anchorage, is sometimes considered Palmer's twin city, since their borders abut. Like Palmer, agriculture is a large part of its economy. Wasilla is one of the Matanuska Valley's earliest American settlements, beginning as a railroad station in 1916. In the intervening years, it has become home to many Anchorage workers who prefer to live and raise their families in more rural surroundings. In 1980-81, Wasilla's population nearly doubled. Its population expansion has been matched by an expansion in shopping centers, malls and other amenities. Among the things to do and see here are:

☒ *Dorothy Page Museum & Visitors Center* — Located on Main Street in the Wasilla Community Hall, the museum is open daily year-round. It features artifacts from the area's mining and agricultural past. Behind the museum are a collection of historic buldings.

☒ *Knik Museum and Mushers' Hall of Fame* — Located on Knik Road, about 13 miles from downtown Wasilla, the museum features information and memorabilia about some of Alaska's most famous mushers and sled dogs.

☒ *Iditarod Winter Carnival* — Held annually in March, the carnival celebrates the Iditarod Sled Dog Race. Wasilla is the second starting point for the race, which attracts mushers and mushing fans from all over the world. Iditarod memorabilia is available from the Iditarod Shop in Wasilla.

For more information, contact the Matanuska-Susitna Convention & Visitor's Bureau, 191 E. Swanson Ave., Suite 201, Wasilla, Alaska 99687, (907) 376-8001.

GATEHOUSE BED & BREAKFAST

P. O. Box 870563
2500 Bogard Road
Wasilla, Alaska 99687
(907) 376-6756; Fax: (907) 376-6756
E-mail: ervin@gatehousealaska.com
Web site: www.gatehousealaska.com
Irene and Clayton Ervin, Hosts

Months Open: Year round
Hours: Check-in 2 p.m.; out 11 a.m.
Credit Cards: VISA, MC
Accommodations: 1 cottage, 1 cabin
Smoking: Outdoors

Children Welcome: Yes
Pets Accommodated: Inquire
Social Drinking: Yes

ROOM RATES
Single: $50 winter; $75 summer
Double: $75 winter; $95 summer
Each additional person: $15
Children under 2 free

Gatehouse Bed & Breakfast is located two miles from Main Street in Wasilla, on the shores of Lake Wasilla. The natural-wood sided cottage stands at the beginning of the driveway to the house, and the small red cabin is 1/4 mile in.

The cottage has two bedrooms and can sleep up to 7 people. It is furnished with a queen-size bed, two single beds, and a full size daybed, and a rollaway bed is available. It also contains a full kitchen, complete bathroom, TV and VCR, fireplace, washer & dryer, and private phone.

The cabin accommodates a maximum of 4 people. It is furnished with a queen-size bed and/or two single beds. It has a kitchenette, wood fireplace, washer & dryer, TV and private phone. It also has a complete bath.

A continental breakfast is provided in the cabin and cottage, consisting of fruit, cold cereal, juice, bagels, muffins or sweet rolls, coffe and tea. Popcorn and breakfast bars are available.

Clayton is a lifelong Alaskan. He was born in Anchorage and moved to the Valley in 1974. Irene hails from Minnesota, but has called Alaska home since 1960. Their three grown children, Tammy, Allan and Paul, sometimes help with the Bed and Breakfast. Clayton and Irene share their home with two dogs, who mostly stay indoors.

SOUTHSHORE BED & BREAKFAST

Box 870723
Wasilla, Alaska 99687
(907) 376-9334; Fax (907) 376-9360
E-mail: sshore@alaska.net
Web page: www.alaskan.com/promos/sshore.html
Helen & Jim Messick, Hosts

Months Open: Year-round   **Children Welcome:** Over 6
Hours: 8 a.m. - 10 p.m.   **Pets Accommodated:** No
Credit Cards: MC, VISA   **Social Drinking:** No
Accommodations: 1 cabin, 1 room   **Smoking:** Outside

ROOM RATES
Single: $70-$85 summer; $50-$75 winter
Double: $80-$95 summer; $65-$85 winter
Each additional person: $20

Southshore Bed & Breakfast is located within a few miles of a medical center, a number of restaurants, shopping centers, golf course, the post office, churches and other facilities. The home offers a quiet, secluded lake-front area for relaxation and enjoyment.

Southshore is surrounded by woods, with 225 feet fronting the shore of two-mile-long Lake Lucille, home to abundant waterfowl. There is a dock for floatplane tie-down and on-site parking for cars and recreational vehicles. The

hosts offer courtesy transportation from and to the Wasilla railroad depot.

A car rental is nearby for those who arrive by train and wish to sightsee during their stay in Wasilla. Flightseeing trips, glacier adventures, whitewater river rafting, guided hikes and fishing trips, highway tours and dog sled adventures can be arranged.

Guests may use the deck overlooking the lake, picnic table and barbecue at the main house, canoe paddle boat, sailboat, dock, bicycles, fish smoker, freezer space, Alaska book and film library, laundry facilities, badminton, computer, fax and printer by arrangement. A complementary fresh fruit and snack basket is offered to all new arrivals. In winter, guests are invited to sit in the main house around a cozy wood stove and sip coffee, Russian tea, hot chocolate or cider.

The cabin, large enough for two adults and a child, is completely modern and offers total privacy, with an outdoor patio, queen-size bed, bathroom with shower, robes, TV, VCR, kitchen, small refrigerator, microwave, toaster oven and coffee pot. A desk is supplied with stationery for your use. A private telephone will enable you to receive calls from friends and family during your stay, and board games are provided. In the main house, there is a room with a double bed, private entrance, private bath, TV, VCR, small refrigerator, microwave oven, coffee pot and desk with stationery.

Breakfast consists of an extensive menu, including sourdough pancakes and waffles. Guests can make their breakfast choice the previous evening.

HUEVOS RANCHEROS

Butter or olive oil	1 c. rancheros sauce
4 corn tortillas	10-16 oz. cooked crumbled sausage
4-8 eggs	4 strips well-done bacon
3/4 c. grated cheddar cheese	sour cream to garnish

Optional: diced sweet red pepper, sliced olives, parsley or cilantro

Soften tortillas in oil/butter. Heat all ingredients except the eggs in the microwave. Fry or poach the eggs. Assemble on a warm plate: 1 tortilla, 1/4 of the sausage, 1-2 eggs, 1/4 c. sauce, 1/4 of the cheese, 1 dollop of sour cream, 1 piece crumbled bacon, desired garnishes. Repeat for remaining servings. Serves 4.

YUKON DON'S
BED & BREAKFAST INN

2221 Yukon Circle
(Mail: 1830 E. Parks Highway 386)
Wasilla, Alaska 99654
(907) 376-7472; Fax (907) 376-7470; 800-478-7472
E-mail: yukondon@alaska.net
Yukon Don and Beverly Tanner, Hosts

Months Open: Year-round
Hours: 24
Credit Cards: MC, VISA
Accommodations: 8 rooms

Children Welcome: All ages
Pets Accommodated: Limited
Social Drinking: Yes
Smoking: Outside

ROOM RATES
Single: $95 private bath; $85 shared bath
Double: $105 private bath; $95 shared bath
Suite w/private bath: $105 single, $115 double
Mini-suite w/private bath: $95 single, $105 double
Executive suite: $125 single, $135 double
Each additional person: $15
Children: 5 and under, free
(7-day cancellation + 20%)

Located one hour from Anchorage on the direct route to Denali Park and Fairbanks, Yukon Don's Bed & Breakfast is "Alaska's most acclaimed B & B inn." It was named "Best of the Best" in 1995, 1996, and 2000 by readers of the valley newspaper, the *Frontiersman*. It was named Alaska's Family Business of the Year for 1994-95, and received the American B & B Association's Excellence Award in 1996. In 1993, it was proclaimed the "Official Bed and Breakfast Home of the city of Wasilla" by the mayor. In 1991 it was named one of the top 50 inns in America.

Each of the inn's eight spacious, comfortable guest rooms is decorated with Alaskana. Guests have their choice of the Iditarod, Fishing, Denali or Southeast rooms or the Matanuska, Klondike or Yukon Executive Suites. There is a phone in each room. Guests can also opt for the semi-rustic A.J. Swanson cabin.

Guests are pampered by relaxing in the Alaska room, complete with Alaskan history library, video library, pool table, cable television and gift shop. The all-glass-view room on the second floor offers the grandest view in the Matanuska Valley, with a 360-degree view of the Chugach and Talkeetna mountain ranges. It features a fireplace, sitting chairs and observation deck. A sauna and an exercise room are also available.

"This is absolutely the best B&B we have yet discovered" said one guest. "The decor is beyond our imagination."

For breakfast, guests can choose from Yukon Don's own expanded continental breakfast bar.

Guests rave about the view from Yukon Don's. As Judge William Hungate, of St. Louis, Missouri, said, "It's like seeing Alaska without leaving the house."

Willow

Willow is one of those Alaska communities that owe their existence to the search for gold. After the California gold rush of 1949, hopeful prospectors began working their way north. It wasn't long until they reached British Columbia, where discoveries at Cassiar encouraged them to proceed even further north. About the same year George Carmack and his companions discovered gold in the soon-to-be-famous Klondike Gold District, prospectors in Alaska discovered gold near Willow. That was 1897, and the town of Willow was born.

In more recent years, Willow achieved some fame as the would-be home to the Alaska Legislature, after voters elected to move the capital from Juneau to a more easily accessible area. Since nobody in either Fairbanks or Anchorage wanted to see the other town get the capital, proponents of the move suggested Willow as a compromise, and the voters went along. However, when it was explained to them how much money it would cost to move the seat of government, voters changed their minds, and Willow remained the cozy little community it had been for so many years.

Willow is on the George Parks Highway, between Wasilla and the turnoff to Talkeetna. Nearby attractions include:

☒ *Hatcher Pass & Independence Mine State Historical Park* — Willow is just south of the western access road to this popular recreation area. Independence Mine was a 200-worker gold mining operation that ran from the early 1900s to 1942, when gold was determined to be a nonstrategic metal and mines were shut down. The visitors' center is located in the former mine manager's home. There is an admission fee and parking fee for the park, but the beautiful drive up to the pass, along the Little Susitna River, costs nothing but the gas to get you there and back.

☒ *Nancy Lake State Recreation Area* — There are 130 lakes in the area and a canoe trail that links a dozen with the Little Susitna River. Fishing is good here. There are also several hiking trails, including a one-mile nature walk.

ALASKAN HOST
BED & BREAKFAST

P. O. Box 38
Willow, Alaska 99688
(907) 495-6800; Fax: (907) 495-6802
E-mail: huston@alaskanhost.com
Web site: www.alaskanhost.com
Kathy and Jim Huston, Hosts

Months Open: Year round
Hours: check-in 3 p.m.; out 11 a.m.
Credit Cards: VISA, MC, DS, AMEX
Accommodations: 3 rooms, 1 suite,
1 1-bedroom apartment

Children Welcome: Yes
Pets Accommodated: No
Social Drinking: In rooms only
Smoking: Outside

ROOM RATES
Single: $55-$60 winter; $65-$75 summer
Double: $65-$80 winter; $75-$95 summer
Apartment: $100/night (ask about weekly/monthly rates)
Each additional person: $10

Alaskan Host Bed & Breakfast is located at Mile 66.5 Parks Highway and half a mile down a private drive. It sits on 200 acres of wooded land, with a private lake for canoeing or paddle-boating. There are hiking and walking trails for two miles around the property and ski trails and snowmachine trails in winter. Inside, the house is all Alaskan, with numer-

ous game mounts and Alaskan animal furs throughout.

All of the guest rooms at the B&B have a theme. The *Whale Room*, which has two queen beds and a private ensuite bath, is decorated with a 14-foot-long mounted baleen and other whale pictures and information. The *Polar Bear Room* is decorated with polar bear pictures and is furnished with a queen-size bed. It shares a bath with the *Loon Room*, which has a queen-size bed and twin bed. The *Moose Suite* features two queen beds, a private hot tub, sauna, in-room bath, small refrigerator and microwave, and a private entrance. The apartment is furnished and has a kitchen area, living room and bedroom. It sleeps up to five people.

Guests are served a full breakfast, which may include moose or caribou sausage, blueberry pancakes, homemade muffins or cinnamon rolls, or ham and eggs, hash browns, homemade bread, and fruit, juice, coffee, tea or hot cocoa. Homemade cookies or cake are usually available.

Jim Huston is a lifetime Alaskan. He has worked for Alaska State Parks for more than 25 years and knows all the great fishing, canoeing and sight seeing places. He has numerous hunting and other Alaska stories to share. Kathy Huston was born in New York, but has been an Alaskan for 22 years. She enjoys working at home, hiking the trails around the property, sewing and crafts, reading, gardening, and talking with her guests. The couple share their home with two dogs. Muffy, a mix of poodle and dachshund, stays mostly indoors, but is a favorite with everybody. Woofer, the black lab outside dog, loves to greet the guests and accompany them on any walks they want to take.

BLUEBERRY FRENCH TOAST

8 eggs	2 c. blueberries
1 1/2 c. milk	1/2 c. brown sugar
1/2 c. half and half	2 T. butter
1 T. vanilla	12 slices bread

Mix together eggs, milk, half and half, and vanilla. Melt butter in a 9" x 13" pan. When butter is melted, sprinkle brown sugar on bottom of pan. Top with 6 slices of bread. Pour 1/2 batter over the bread and spread 1 c. of blueberries over all. Repeat the layers. Cover and refrigerate overnight. In the morning remove from refrigerator and let stand at room temperature while oven is being heated to 350°. Bake for 45 minutes or until a knife inserted in center comes out clean. Maple syrup or powered sugar is great on top.

Interior Alaska

- Fairbanks

Interior Alaska

Interior Alaska, the vast heartland that forms the center of our state, is a huge, sparsely populated area that spans an area larger than the state of Texas. Extending from above the Arctic Circle on the north to the Alaska Range on the south and from the Canadian border on the east to about 100 miles inland from the Bering Sea on the west, it is filled with spectacular mountains, magnificent rivers and grand vistas. Through it runs the mighty Yukon, at 2,300 miles long the largest river in Alaska and the fifth largest in North America, as well as the second largest river in Alaska, the Kuskokwim. On the south, Denali, North America's tallest mountain, looms over the plateau that forms the Interior. It is a land of extremes, with summer temperatures reaching near 100 degrees Fahrenheit and winter temperatures often plunging to -60 degrees or lower.

The second largest city in Alaska, Fairbanks, is the population center of this area. Other, much smaller, communities lie strung out along the highways north and south and along the rivers. Many of the river communities are home to Alaska's Athabaskan Indians, the original inhabitants of Interior Alaska.

Besides unparalleled opportunities for sightseeing, Interior Alaska offers a myriad of recreational opportunities including mountain climbing, hiking, camping, river rafting, kayaking, canoeing, fishing, skiing, snowmachining, dog mushing, hunting, trapping. Bus tours to and through Denali National Park, flightseeing throughout the area, and car trips to hot springs, to the Arctic Circle or other unique destinations, and fly-in trips to remote cabins and villages are among the other enjoyments available to visitors.

Fairbanks

Fairbanks came to life in 1903, after gold was discovered along nearby creeks. It was established as a trading post for area gold miners by E.T. Barnette. By 1910, the population of the town and the creeks beyond had reached 11,000 and Fairbanks was chosen as the northern end of Alaska's first highway, the Richardson, which, although it began as a trail rather than a cleared roadway, connected it to Valdez, 368 miles to the south. The town was also chosen as the site for the state's first university campus. It is the supply point and transportation hub for Interior and northern communities.

Attractions for visitors include:

☒ *University of Alaska and University Museum* — Both facilities offer special programs and tours during summer. The Georgeson Botanical Gardens offer a bright display of northern flowers. The museum features exhibits of Native culture and prehistoric Alaska.

☒ *Alaskaland* — The state's only "theme park," Alaskaland is set in the gold rush days. Highlights include a miniature railroad, restored sternwheeler, museum and historic houses.

☒ *Walking Tour* — Fairbanks Convention and Visitors Bureau offers a free, guided tour of the historic downtown. Brochures and maps for self-guided tours are available at the visitor center.

☒ *Golden Days* — This annual July celebration of the discovery of gold near Fairbanks features a parade, dance, races, contests, outdoor concerts, pancake breakfasts and a flower show.

☒ *World Eskimo-Indian Olympics* — Alaska Natives from around the state gather at the University of Alaska campus in July each year to compete in traditional games and dances. The event is commemorated in a book called *Heartbeat.*

☒ *Tanana Valley State Fair* — Held each August, the fair offers arts and crafts, carnival rides, food, large-vegetable contests and more.

☒ *Northern Lights* — Fairbanks winter skies offer some of the most spectacular displays of the aurora borealis seen anywhere, attracting visitors from all over the globe.

For more information contact the Fairbanks Convention and Visitors Bureau, 550 First Ave., Fairbanks, AK 99701, (907) 456-5774.

AAAA CARE BED & BREAKFAST

557 Fairbanks Street
Fairbanks AK 99709
(907) 479-2447, (800) 478-2705; Fax (907) 479-2484
Web page: www.alaskan.com/aaaacare
Pat Obrist, Host

Months open: Year round   **Children welcome:** Yes
Hours: 24   **Pets accommodated:** On approval
Credit cards: VISA, MC, DS, AMEX   **Social drinking:** Yes
Accommodations: 6 rooms   **Smoking:** Outside
Guest Home for military (TLA)—Long term stay

ROOM RATES*
Single: $99-$125/$150 summer, $65-$85/$99 winter
Double: $99-$125/$150 summer, $65-$85/$99 winter
Each additional person: $35 adult, $25 child
(*Please add 8% bed tax)

AAAA Care Bed & Breakfast is a spacious log home located near the University of Alaska Fairbanks, the airport, railroad, and the George Parks Highway. It is only minutes from downtown Fairbanks. Transportation to or from the airport or train station is available.

The B&B facility is a newly built, more than 3,000-square-feet, addition to the main house. It has a private entry, eight rooms with half or full baths, phone, cable VCR/TV and privacy locks, as well as five full baths, living room and kitchen. Two rooms have king-size beds, six rooms have queen-size beds and/or twin beds, one has a queen-size bed and two twin beds. The last room is perfect for families. It has a queen-size bed and bunk beds, with a double on the bottom and a twin on top. There are decks all around the new unit, for guest use only. Laundry facilities are available for a small fee. The B&B also offers wonderful northern lights viewing, Pat says.

A full breakfast is served and may include blueberry or banana pancakes, French toast, bacon, sausage, or eggs. Special breakfasts can be prepared by request. Dinner is also available, for $8 per person, for guests who would like to join the family at table.

Host Pat Obrist is joined by her two children in her efforts to provide a warm welcome and comfortable stay for her guests. Mary and Tyler, ages 18 and 17, "are my total helpers from breakfast to check-out," Pat says. Mary, in addition, is able to give private tours of Fairbanks for a per-person fee of $35 and up.

The family shares their home with two small dogs: toy poodle Cody and gramma-terry mix Linda. While the dogs are not allowed into the guest area, they love greeting guests. "You might even get a visit from a passing moose," Pat says.

AH, ROSE MARIE
DOWNTOWN BED & BREAKFAST

302 Cowles Street
Fairbanks, Alaska 99701
(907) 456-2040; Fax (907) 456-6193
Web page: www.akpub.com/akbbrv/ahrose.html
John E. Davis and Tyla the Cat, Hosts

Months Open: Year-round	**Children Welcome:** All ages
Hours: 24	**Pets Accommodated:** No
Credit Cards: None	**Social Drinking:** Yes
Accommodations: 5 rooms	**Smoking:** Outside

ROOM RATES*
Single: $60 + tax
Double: $75 + tax
(*Winter discounts and family rooms available)

Very centrally located "on the edge of downtown, three blocks south of the river," Ah, Rose Marie is a refurbished 1928 home. The house has an enclosed front porch, a downstairs guest parlor, and a picnic area. Guests are permitted full use of the house and grounds. The house is gleaming white with bright red trim. Gorgeous flowers abound.

John serves a full, hearty breakfast, including homemade bread, pastries and jams, fresh fruit, cereal, egg dishes, and fresh-brewed coffee or tea. Breakfast is served in the dining room or on the enclosed front porch. Tea and cookies are available at any time, and there is a picnic table for use on warm Fairbanks days.

"At Ah, Rose Marie we offer extraordinary hospitality and truly wonderful breakfasts served family style. Guests are free to come and go at any hour," says John.

B & R BED & BREAKFAST

640 Gradelle Street
Fairbanks, Alaska 99709
(907) 479-3335; Fax (907) 479-7232
E-mail: paghsbed@mosquitonet.com
Web site: www.mosquitonet.com/~paghsbed
Rose and Bob Pagh, Hosts

Months Open: Year round	**Children Welcome:** Yes
Hours: 8 a.m.-9 p.m.	**Pets Accommodated:** No
Credit Cards: VISA, MS, DS, AMEX	**Social Drinking:** Yes
Accommodations: 3 rooms	**Smoking:** No

ROOM RATES
Single w/shared bath: $35 winter, $50 summer
Single w/private bath: $40 winter, $55 summer
Double w/shared bath: $45 winter, $65 summer
Double w/private bath: $50 winter, $75 summer
Each additional person: $10
Children under 10 free

B & R Bed and Breakfast is conveniently located just one-quarter mile from the University of Alaska campus, and a mile and a half from the Parks Highway. It is a split-level home, white with black trim. There is a large yard, with birch and spruce trees and a deck with a barbeque. Inside, the living and dining rooms are carved teakwood with an oriental design. The kitchen is available for guest use. Bikes are available as well. Guests who prefer a more relaxing pastime can browse through the library of videos and books about Alaska.

The rooms are decorated with an Alaska flair. The *Scrimshaw Room* has a queen bed with private bath. The *Bev Doolittle Room* has a queen bed with shared bath. And the *Doug Lindstrom Room* has a double bed and twin bed, with a shared bath.

Breakfast is modified continental, with fresh fruit, muffins, bagels, croissants and a large variety of cereals, as well as coffee, tea and juices. Fresh fruit, sodas and juice are available at all times.

The Paghs have lived in Alaska since 1970. They have seven grown sons and many grandchildren. Bob originally came from Oregon and Rose was born in Germany. They share their home with two outside dogs and a white rabbit. None of the animals are allowed into the guest area.

Among the many things for visitors to do in the area include visiting the Riverboat Discovery, the University Museum, and the historic downtown area. There are also three working mines in the area. The Paghs are happy to make reservations for any or all of these sights for their guests.

FOX CREEK BED AND BREAKFAST

2498 Elliott Highway (1.1 Mile)
Fairbanks, Alaska 99712
(907) 457-5494; Fax (907) 457-5464
E-mail: foxcreek@ptialaska.net
Web page: www.ptialaska.net/~foxcreek
Arna & Jeff Fay, Hosts

Months Open: Year-round
Hours: 24
Credit Cards: None
Accommodations: 2 rooms

Children Welcome: Yes
Pets Accommodated: Yes
Social Drinking: Yes
Smoking: Outside

ROOM RATES
Summer: Shared bath, $55 single, $68 double
Summer: Private bath, $85 single, $98 double
Winter: private bath only, $55 single, $68 double
Each additional person: $15
Children: Under 5 free

Fox Creek Bed and Breakfast is 12 miles north of downtown Fairbanks, in the old mining town of Fox. The superinsulated, cedar-sided house has a large deck, and its wooded location gives a quiet, secluded, rustic feeling. The aurora borealis is frequently seen between September and April, and wildlife sightings are a regular occurrence. In Fox are several excellent restaurants, gold panning, gold dredge tours, and the world famous Howling Dog Saloon.

The home has two spacious guest rooms. The upstairs room, with shared bath, can accommodate three persons comfortably. The downstairs room can accommodate four or five and has a 3/4 private bath and private entrance. Each room has a futon sofa and TV/VCR. All guests are invited to use the cozy living room. Video rentals are available nearby in Fox, and a large garage may be used for minor repairs.

The Fays serve a hearty Alaska-style breakfast featuring pancakes or muffins made with local blueberries, Belgian waffles, fancy French toast (the Fays' special recipe), eggs, reindeer sausage, fresh fruit, and fresh-ground coffee. For guests who prefer a continental-style breakfast, that is available too.

Arna, who runs Fox Creek, is a lifelong Alaskan, born and raised in Fairbanks. Jeff, a videographer and editor and media specialist, was born in

Anchorage, but has lived in Fairbanks since 1967. Both Arna and Jeff enjoy skiing and snowmobiling in winter. Arna keeps many plants, several fish tanks and a terrarium with frogs, newts and toads. She also enjoys feeding a wide variety of wild birds at several feeders. They have a dog and a cockatiel bird as house pets. Jeff is an avid motorcyclist in summer.

FOX CREEK FANCY FRUITY FRENCH TOAST

1 loaf of bread	1/2 tsp. cinnamon
4 eggs	1/2 tsp. vanilla (optional)
1/3 c. milk	8 oz. fruit-flavored cream cheese
	(strawberry or pineapple)

Mix eggs, milk, cinnamon and vanilla in shallow bowl. Make cream-cheese sandwiches with bread and cream cheese, then dip repeatedly in egg mixture until all eggs are absorbed. Brown in a little butter or bacon fat on a medium-hot griddle. Sprinkle with powdered sugar and serve with bacon, ham or sausage, warm syrup and fresh fruit. Makes 4 servings.

GENI'S BED & BREAKFAST

P.O. Box 10352
Fairbanks, Alaska 99710
(907) 488-4136
E-mail: genisbb@mosquitonet.com
Web site: www.bedandbreakfast.com
George and Nila Lyle

Months Open: May 15-Sept. 15
Hours: 24; check-in 4 p.m.
Credit Cards: None
Accommodations: 3 rooms

Chiildren Welcome: Yes
Pets Accommodated: No
Social Drinking: Yes
Smoking: On deck only

ROOM RATES
Shared bath: $75
Private bath: $85

Geni's Bed and Breakfast is a cedar, prow-shaped home about 15 miles from downtown Fairbanks, just off the Chena Hot Springs Road. The house has lots of windows, for a maximum of light and potential moose sightings. Guests can relax or picnic on the deck. Inside, the house is decorated country-style, with comfortable furniture in earth shades and lots of silk flower arrangements, one of Nila's many talents. There is a spiral staircase and a sitting room with organ, TV, radio, and VCR.

Guests have their choice of three rooms. One is a large room with

private bath, bedside table, vanity, rocking chair, chest of drawers, and two queen-size beds with quilted coverlets. The remaining two rooms share a bath. Each has a queen bed with quilt, night table, reading table and chair. Walls and tables are decorated with silk flower wreaths and arrangements.

George and Nila serve a full breakfast, which consists of coffee, tea, juice, homemade bread and jellies, sausage or bacon, fresh fruit dish, and a main dish such as waffles, pancakes or breakfast pie. Breakfast is served in a sunny, glass dining room. Coffee and tea are always available.

George is a homesteader and house builder who refinishes furniture. Nila is a retired elementary school teacher who enjoys working with silk flowers. The couple works together producing craft items for their business, Geni's Critters and Crafts.

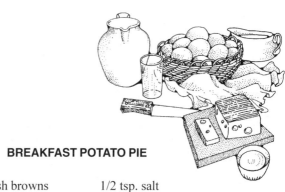

BREAKFAST POTATO PIE

6-oz. pkg. hash browns
1 green onion or scallion
1 qt. hot water
5 eggs
1/2 c. cottage cheese
1 c. shredded Swiss cheese

1/2 tsp. salt
1/8 tsp. pepper
4 drops hot sauce
5 slices cooked ham, crumbled
paprika (for color)

Cover hash browns with water. Let stand 10 minutes, then drain. Beat eggs, add potatoes and remaining ingredients, except paprika. Pour into 10-inch pie pan. Sprinkle with paprika. Cover and refrigerate overnight. In the morning, place in cold oven, uncovered. Bake at 350° for 35 minutes or until potatoes are tender.

7 GABLES INN

P.O. Box 80488
Fairbanks, Alaska 99708-0488
(907) 479-0751; Fax (907) 479-2229
E-mail: gables7@alaska.net
Web page: 7gablesinn.com
Paul & Leicha Welton, Hosts

Months Open: Year-round
Hours: 24
Credit Cards: AMEX, DC, DS, MC, VISA
Accommodations: 9 rooms, 6 apts.

Children Welcome: Yes
Pets Accommodated: Outdoors, and in garage
Social Drinking: Yes
Smoking: Restricted

ROOM RATES
Single: $85-$110 summer; $50-$60 winter
Double: $85-$120 summer; $50-$75 winter
Suites: $100-$150 summer; $75-$95 winter
Each additional person: $10
Children: $10

Located between the airport and the University of Alaska, 7 Gables Inn is a 10,000-square-foot former fraternity house. The inn was designed and built by host Paul Welton, and among its unique features are a floral solarium entrance, antique stained-glass-decorated foyer with indoor waterfall, and cathedral ceilings.

Amenities include private Jacuzzi baths, color cable TV/VCRs and private phone lines in each room, conference and banquet facilities, laundry facilities and bikes and canoes for guest use.

Accommodations range from single rooms to two- and three-room suites. Some rooms have twin beds, others have queen-size beds. One suite has two queen-size beds and a trundle daybed; others have a king-size bed and a queen-size hide-a-bed. All the rooms have private showers/ baths, either in the room or outside the room. Nine of the rooms and all of the suites have private Jacuzzis. Each room is equipped with a desk, cable TV/VCR and private phone. Some suites have fireplaces.

7 Gables is known for its fabulous breakfasts. Leicha is a great cook who enjoys collecting cook books. Each morning, she serves a full gourmet breakfast that includes a variety of hot entrees, muffins, breads, coffee cakes, fruit, cereal, juice and coffee or tea. A typical morning's menu might include blintz souffle, apricot kugel, bagels and cream cheese, rugulah, latkes and charoseth. Another morning might bring stuffed French toast, sausage and apple balls, elegant scrambled eggs, strawberry frappes and a fruit mixture of bananas, kiwi fruit and strawberries. Each breakfast is an adventure in dining.

In the "off" hours, guests may help themselves to soda from the guest refrigerator, bread, peanut butter and jelly, and in-room mints.

Summer attractions include the Riverboat Discovery, the University Museum, Ester Gold Camp, Alaskaland, Gold Dredge #8, the Pumphouse Restaurant, canoeing and biking. In winter, guests may enjoy dog-sled rides, cross-country and downhill skiing, the international ice carver's competition, and northern lights viewing.

CAPPUCCINO CHIP MUFFINS
WITH CHOCOLATE CREAM CHEESE ESPRESSO SPREAD

Muffins:

2 c. flour	1/2 tsp. ground cinnamon
3/4 c. sugar	1 c. milk, scalded and cooled
2-1/2 tsp. baking powder	1/2 c. butter, melted and cooled
2 tsp. instant espresso coffee powder	1 egg, lightly beaten
	1 tsp. vanilla extract
1/2 tsp. salt	3/4 c. semi-sweet chocolate mini chips

Preheat oven to 375°. Grease 12 four-oz. or 6 8-oz. muffin tins. In a large bowl, stir together flour, sugar, baking powder, espresso coffee powder, salt and cinnamon. In another, medium, bowl, stir together until blended milk, butter, egg and vanilla. Make a well in the center of the dry ingredients, add milk mixture and stir just to combine. Fold in chips. Spoon batter into prepared muffin tins. Bake 15-20 minutes, or until top springs back when touched. Turn muffins out onto wire rack. Serve with a generous amount of Chocolate Espresso Cream Cheese Spread.

Spread:

4 oz. cream cheese, softened	1 T. sugar
1 sq. (1 oz) semi-sweet chocolate, melted and cooled	1/2 tsp. vanilla
	1/2 tsp. instant espresso coffee powder

Place cream cheese, chocolate, sugar, vanilla and espresso in small bowl and blend thoroughly, until smooth and of a consistent color. Allow to soften at room temperature for 10 minutes before serving.

UEBERNACHTUNG UND FRUEHSTUECK BED & BREAKFAST

2402 Cowles Street
Fairbanks, Alaska 99701
(907) 455-7958; Fax (907) 452-7958
E-mail: 103707.2401@compuserve.com
Web Site: www.akpub.com/akbbrv/ueber.html
Rob and Sylvia Harris, Hosts

Months Open: Year round
Hours: Check-in 4 p.m.-12; out 11 a.m.
Credit Cards: None
Accommodations: 2 rooms

Children Welcome: Inquire
Pets Accommodated: No
Social Drinking: Yes
Smoking: No

ROOM RATES
Room with shared bath: $55
Room with private bath: $65
Each additional person: $20
Children under 4 free; 4-8 $10; 8 and up $20

This colorful B & B is centrally located, just five minutes from downtown Fairbanks, 10 minutes from the airport, and 4 blocks from the highway. The house sits on 1/2 acre, just across the street from the baseball field. It's an older house, farmhouse style, with a nice mixture of old and

new furniture and lots of built-ins. A plus for guests is that both English and German are spoken here.

Guests have their choice of two rooms. One has a queen-size bed, built-in dresser and private bath. The other shares a bath, and has a queen-size bed and twin bed, as well as a built-in dresser.

A full breakfast comes with the room. It consists of eggs cooked to order, bacon or sasuage, muffins, cereal, toast, butter, homemade jams, including German plum, apricot and Alaska blueberry, coffee, tea, milk and orange juice.

Rob hails originally from Florida and now works as a service technician in the propane business. Sylvia is from Germany and owns her own cleaning buisness. The have been in Alaska since 1991. They have a 16-year old son who lives with them. They also share their home with two dogs — a lab/husky mix and a lab/golden retriever mix — a grey cat and a bird. The dogs are obedience trained and are not allowed in bedrooms. The cat roams the house.

"You will be treated as a very special guest," Rob and Sylvia say. "If you don't want to go out at night, we have a lot of movies to watch, games to play, or music from the '50s, '60s and '70s, as well as country to listen to. Or you can watch Deutsche Welle courtesty of our satellite dish."

During the day, there are many activities nearby to occupy and entertain visitors, including gold panning, river rafting, hot air ballooning, taking a ride on the Riverboat Discovery, or running out to Chena Hot Springs for a soak in the springs.

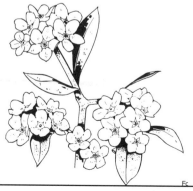

Southeast Alaska

- Gustavus
- Juneau-Douglas
- Sitka
- Yakutat

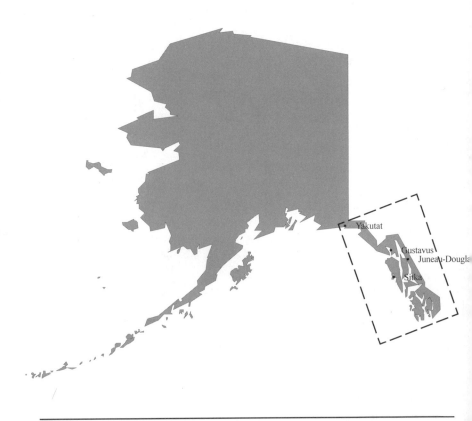

Southeast Alaska

Southeast Alaska, also known as the panhandle, lies in what Alaskans like to call the banana belt of Alaska. As the name implies, the warmest winter temperatures in Alaska are found in this region. A wonderland of emerald islands, towering spruce and cedar trees, sparkling glaciers and soaring peaks, Southeast is a tourist's delight. In fact, tourists have been visiting the area since America purchased Alaska from Russia in 1867.

Russia's legacy is evident at Sitka, one of the jewel-like communities that dot this 400-mile long greenbelt. History is never far from view here. At Ketchikan and other communities, tall totems testify to the legacy of Southeast's original inhabitants, the Tlingit and Haida Indians. In Juneau

and Skagway, relics from
found. At Haines,
presence is seen in the
Fort William H. Seward.

Most people come
the scenery and the wild-
away disappointed. Any-
you can expect to see
mammals. Eagles soar
and the Chilkat River
largest winter concentra-
seen anywhere. Sitka
and black bears, sheep
mammals that may be
summer, the rivers run
salmon.

There is a wide va-

the gold rush can be
America's earliest military
renovated buildings of old

to Southeast Alaska for
life, and they don't go
time you're on the water,
whales and other marine
through the skies of Sitka,
near Haines boasts the
tion of bald eagles to be
black-tailed deer, brown
and goats are among the
seen in the area. And in the
rife with spawning

riety of activities that can
be enjoyed by visitors to Southeast Alaska — something for nearly every taste, in fact. Outdoor recreationists can fish, hunt, boat, kayak, camp, hike, climb or canoe. For the "culturally" inclined, there are theatrical presentations and other performances, as well as a number of art galleries and museums.

A PUFFIN'S BED & BREAKFAST LODGE

P.O. Box 3
Gustavus, Alaska 99826-0003
(907) 697-2260; in Alaska (800) 478-2258
Fax (907) 697-2258
E-mail: sandy@puffintravel.com
Web site: www.puffintravel.com
Sandy & Chuck Schroth, Hosts

Months Open: May 1 - Sept. 15
Hours: 24
Credit Cards: None
Accommodations: 6 cabins and Puffin Lodge

Children Welcome: Yes
Pets Accommodated: Yes
Social Drinking: Yes
Smoking: Outside

ROOM RATES*
Single w/private bath: $95
Double w/private bath: $95-$125
Each additional person: $25
Children: 2-12, $10; under 2 free
(* All are guest cabins which sleep 3 to 5 people)

A Puffin's Bed and Breakfast is within walking distance of restaurants, grocery stores, the community park and river fishing spots in central Gustavus. The Schroths will meet you on arrival and give you a tour of the

town on the way to their seven-acre homestead.

Puffin's offers six modern cabins with comfortable beds, all attractively decorated with Alaska art prints and crafts. Their newest addition is the Glacier Bear Rental House, a complete house sitting on two forested acres. It sleeps six. The cabins — named Salmon, Halibut, Orca, Sea Otter, Whale and Glacier Bear — can comfortably accommodate from three to six people. Two cabins have sparkling clean private baths, located in a separate building just down a flower-bordered path, while the other four have attached baths. An outdoor barbecue and picnic area is also available for guest use. One cabin and Puffin Lodge are wheelchair accessible, and the lodge has a dining and social area, handicap-access bath, library full of Alaskana books, musical instruments and a private conference room.

Breakfast is served at Puffin Lodge anytime before 9 a.m. and may include delicious waffles, pancakes, French toast or eggs and toast with local jams and syrups. The coffee pot is always on at the lodge and there is a hot pot and coffee, tea and hot chocolate in each cabin.

The Schroths also operate Puffin Travel, a year-round, full travel service, and can set you up with reservations for sight-seeing, fishing, tour boats, accommodations and travel.

"A Puffin's Bed and Breakfast offers itinerary planning in addition to our bed and breakfast, emphasizing a peaceful, successful, genuine Alaskan experience," Chuck and Sandy say.

PUFFIN'S FRENCH TOAST

2 eggs	1/2 tsp. nutmeg
2 c. milk	Sourdough bread slices
1 tsp. cinnamon	

Mix first four ingredients with whisk. Dip both sides of bread into egg mixture; fry in margarine until light brown on both sides. Microwave one minute, or until done. Sift confectioners' sugar over French toast and serve with fresh fruit.

Juneau–Douglas

Juneau, Alaska's capital, was founded in the 1880s when Joe Juneau and Dick Harris discovered gold in a nearby creek. The two biggest mines, the Treadwell and the Alaska-Juneau Mine, together produced about $154 million in gold before they were shut down in World War II.

Douglas is a short drive away, directly across Gastineau Channel. The two towns make up one of the most scenic "cities" in America. As state capital, major commercial fishing port and tourism center, Juneau is usually bustling with activity, while Douglas is much slower-paced. Visitor attractions include:

☒ *Alaska State Museum* — The museum offers a complete display of Alaska's history, from the Russian fur-trade era to the trans-Alaska pipeline, as well as Alaska Native artifacts and an eagle's nest.

☒ *Art Galleries* — Downtown Juneau is a veritable treasure trove of art. More than a dozen fine-art galleries cluster within walking distance of one another and make a wonderful way to spend a day.

☒ *Capitol Building* — Built in 1931, the Capitol houses the legislature and governor's office. With its extensive marble work and painted murals, it's worth a visit.

☒ *Governor's Mansion* — While not open to the public, the Governor's Mansion is worth a peek from the outside, whether you are walking or driving on Calhoun Avenue.

☒ *Eaglecrest Ski Area* — On Douglas Island, Eaglecrest is popular in summer and winter and offers tremendous views.

☒ *Mendenhall Glacier* — This glacier, which lies 13 miles northwest of Juneau, can be reached by paved road and has a visitors center with an audio-visual room.

☒ *Perseverance Theatre* — A professional theater company, Perseverance offers a full season of plays in the winter and "The Lady Lou Revue" during the summer.

For more information, contact the Juneau Convention & Visitors Bureau, 134 Third Street, Juneau, AK 99801, (907) 586-2201.

SERENITY INN LUXURY
BED & BREAKFAST AND GARDENS

P. O. Box 210902
Auke Bay, Alaska 99821
(907) 789-2330 or (800) 877-5369; Fax, phone first
E-mail: serenity@ptialaska.net
Web site: ptialaska.net/~serenity
Marilyn and Ed Linsell, Hosts

Months Open: All year
Hours: Check-in 3 p.m., out noon
Credit Cards: MC, VISA, AMEX
Accommodations: 3 rooms

Children Welcome: Yes
Pets Accommodated: No
Social Drinking:
Smoking: No

ROOM RATES
Summer: w/shared bath, $99; w/private bath, $129
Winter: Single or Double: $69
Each additional person: $10

Serenity Inn is a custom, contemporary, A-frame, cedar home, located on Auke Bay, close to the University of Alaska Southeast, the State Ferry terminal, airport, and Mendenhall Glacier. The house has vaulted ceilings and outdoor decks surrounded by perennial and annual gardens.

There is a hot tub on the deck. The house is tastefully decorated throughout in shades of forest green, dark blue and maroon and natural cedar. The

house is meticulously cleaned daily and there are no pets on premises, so people plagued by allergies can breathe easily.

Two guest rooms on the main floor, the *Forest* and *Garden Rooms*, share a bath and a living room. They are furnished with queen size bed. The *Treetop Room*, on the second floor, is a large room with vaulted ceiling, custom windows, sitting area, and private bath. It comes with a king-size bed. All rooms have a desk and TV/VCR.

Breakfast is full and scrumptious. It may consist of gingerbread pancakes served with hot scalloped apples and maple whipped cream and syrup and smoked sausage, as well as hot beverages, juice, and fresh fruit. "My guests don't need lunch!" Marilyn says.

In case they are hungry by afternoon, however, Marilyn puts out home-made cookes, bar cookies, brownies, chips, pretzels and self-serve popcorn every afternoon and evening. Hot and cold beverages are always available.

Marilyn and Ed came to Alaska on vacation in 1991. "Because of the beautiful scenery of the ocean, the mountains and the forests, and the wonderful people we met, we knew we had to move here," Marilyn said. "We enjoy helping our guests plan their adventures so they can experience the splendor of this magnificent part of the world."

Activities the Linsells recommend include hiking, kayaking, fishing, flightseeing, boat tours to Tracy Arm Fjord, boat tours for wildlife and whale watching, helicopter glacier hiking and dog sledding, bicycling, rafting, picnicking, bird watching, beach combing, shopping, dining, checking out local and Native art work, the theater, concerts in the park, a trip to the botanical gardens, a tram ride up Mt. Roberts, visits to the salmon hatcheries, and, of course, to the museums.

Sitka

Sitka, located on Baranof Island, southwest of Juneau, is Southeast Alaska's oldest western city. It was settled in the early 1800s by representatives of the Russian-America Company, who ousted the original Tlingit inhabitants and made the new town the capital of Russian America. The Russian and Tlingit heritage is amply evident throughout town, from the onion-dome Russian Orthodox church in the center of town to the totems lining the trail through Sitka National Historical Park. Mount Edgecumbe School, a boarding school for Alaska Native students, is situated here, as is Sheldon Jackson College. The town is reached by commercial air carrier or by boat, including the Alaska state ferry. Attractions include:

☒ *Alaska Day Festival* — Held October 15-18, the festival commemorates the transfer of Alaska from Russia to the United States and features a ball and costume wearing.

☒ *Sitka Summer Music Festival* — The festival, in June, features chamber music concerts on Tuesday and Friday evenings in the Centennial Building. Musicians come from around the world to perform in what has become Alaska's most prestigious concert series. The back wall of the building is glass and offers a fabulous panoramic view of the water, islands and soaring eagles.

☒ *New Archangel Dancers* — Costumed folk dancers perform authentic Russian dances in the Centennial building almost daily in summer, and certainly whenever the ferry or cruise ships are in port.

☒ *Sheldon Jackson Museum* — The museum, located on the college campus, features one of the finest collections of Native artwork in the state, much of it gathered by the missionary for whom it is named. Sheldon Jackson was Alaska's first commissioner of education.

☒ *Sitka National Historical Park* — The park, situated on the site of the original Tlingit fort, features a visitor center with programs and exhibits of Indian and Russian artifacts, as well as demonstrations of traditional Tlingit art. A self-guided walk winds through the park to the fort site and battleground.

For more information, contact the Sitka Convention and Visitors Bureau at P.O. Box 1226, Sitka, AK 99835, (907) 747-5940, fax (907) 747-3739.

ALASKA OCEAN VIEW
BED & BREAKFAST

1101 Edgecumbe Drive
Sitka, Alaska 99835
(907) 747-8310, (888) 811-6870; Fax (907) 747-3440
E-mail: alaskaoceanview@gci.net
Web page: www.sitka-alaska-lodging.com
Bill & Carole Denkinger, Hosts

Months Open: Year-round	**Children Welcome:** All ages
Hours: 24	**Pets Accommodated:** Inquire
Credit Cards: AMEX, MC, VISA	**Social Drinking:** In rooms only
Accommodations: 3 rooms	**Smoking:** No

ROOM RATES*
Range: $69-$149
Sales and bed taxes not included in rates
*A two-night or greater stay requested during peak season
(Generally May-September and certain other peak dates)

Alaska Ocean View Bed & Breakfast is one block from the seashore and Tongass National Forest, the northernmost temperate rainforest in the world. The B&B is within walking distance of the central business district, harbors, trails, schools, galleries, shops and historic attractions such as St. Michael's Russian Cathedral.

The three-story, Alaska-style, red cedar B&B's attractive interior has the look and feel of a country inn in miniature, with only a quarter of the building visible from the street's main entrance. The B& B's large windows and its large deck are perfect for enjoying the stunning ocean and mountain views, and its location in a quiet, safe, residential area offers plenty of complimentary off-street parking and convenient drive-up access to the first two floors.

The B&B is beautifully landscaped with lush, terraced rock gardens, graced with winding rustic rock stairs leading down to a lawn bordered by a forested area complete with edible wild berries and a small waterfall. On the back patio, guests find the hot tub spa soothes the body and viewing eagles from the hot tub soothes the soul.

The common area's cozy, red cedar parlor with vaulted ceiling and large windows invites enjoying the view, visiting with other guests or curling up in front of the parlor fireplace with a great book from the extensive library.

Guest rooms are named after Alaska wildflowers and contain a coffee maker, Bose CD/radio entertainment center, 55-channel cable TV, VCR, phones, mini-refrigerator, mini-microwaves, king or queen-size bed, table and chairs, goose down comforter and pillows (non-allergenic available). Luxury robes and slippers are provided. Rooms also have easy chairs or a sofa. In addition, one room offers a fireplace and a whirlpool bath, and another offers a fireplace and a sofa.

A generous, delicious breakfast is served buffet-style, overlooking the water. Guests can sit where they choose, either in the cozy breakfast nook, the charming dining room, alfresco on the deck, or in the intimacy of their room. Breakfast offerings include fresh fruit in season, freshly ground locally roasted coffee, juice, cereals, and an entree such as gourmet egg dishes, stuffed French toast, specialty waffles, Alaska sourdough pancakes with blueberries, filled crepes, smoked salmon, crab quiche, Russian blini, and a variety of breads and breakfast pastries. Complimentary snacks are available later in the day, including fresh baked goodies such as chocolate chip cookies, Russian teacakes, or Indian fry bread. Coffee, tea, hot-spiced cider, Russian tea and hot chocolate are available 24 hours a day, along with microwave popcorn and a variety of munchies.

Guests can take the airport or ferry shuttle to the B&B for about $3.50.

Yakutat

Yakutat is a coastal community of about 500 people, nestled on the Gulf of Alaska, where Southeast joins the main body of Alaska. Originally a winter village for Tlingit Indians, the area became the site of one of Russian America's first agricultural settlements, an experiment that ultimately failed. These days, the community is supported by a lively fishing industry. In 1986, the community came to national attention when nearby Hubbard Glacier grew so fast it closed the mouth of a fjord and trapped numbers of seals and porpoises in the lake it created. The Malaspina Glacier, the largest in North America, can be seen from town. During the Klondike gold rush, miners seeking an American route to the gold fields attempted to cross the Malaspina, but few survived.

THE BLUE HERON INN

Box 254
Yakutat, Alaska 99689-0254
(907) 784-3287; Fax (907) 784-3603
John & Fran Latham, Hosts

Months Open: Year-round
Hours: 6 a.m. - 10 p.m.
Credit Cards: None
Accommodations: 4 rooms

Children Welcome: Yes
Pets accommodated: No
Social Drinking: Yes
Smoking: Outside

ROOM RATES
January - July: $90 single; $120 double
August - October 15: $120 double or single;
each additional person, $60
October 16 - December: $90 single; $120 double

The Blue Heron Inn is located on Yakutat Bay, five miles from the airport and a five-minute walk from the scenic boat harbor. The newly constructed home has cedar shingles on the outside, and inside it sports a marble fireplace and wooden floors. Original sporting art and many antique decoys are displayed throughout the house.

Guests have their choice of four rooms, two with private entrances and private baths. The *Heron's Nest* features a double bed, three single beds, a private bath, private entrance, kitchenette with sink, microwave and refrigerator, and a telephone. The *Captain's Room* features a double bed, a single bed, a private bath, private entrance, VCR, and telephone. The *Raven's Nest* has a double brass bed, lace curtains, telephone and it shares a bath. The *Crow's Nest* has a single bed, shared bath, radio, telephone and window seat. Down comforters and flannel sheets keep guests snug, even in cool weather.

Guests also have use of a freezer and refrigerator, as well as a fish-cleaning table for successful anglers.

Fran has been a camp cook for over 25 years and serves a varied breakfast consisting of fruit, coffee or tea, pancakes, waffles, hot cereal, muffins, coffee cake and, occasionally, bacon or sausage. Coffee or tea is available throughout the day.

In her spare time, Fran likes to weave and garden. John is a master guide and outfitter and likes to share stories about his 28 years of hunting and fishing in the Interior and Southeast Alaska. Teen-age daughters Anna and Rachel help with the cooking and day-to-day chores. Dusty, a friendly Chesapeake Bay retriever, is part of the family and will greet guests at the door.

SWEDISH PANCAKE

4 eggs	1 qt. milk
2 c. unsifted flour	1/2 lb. butter

Beat eggs; add milk and flour and continue beating with mixer. Preheat oven to 425°. Place butter in a 10-inch cast-iron skillet and melt in the oven. Pour egg mixture into skillet and bake 35-40 minutes. Serve with sour cream, hot sliced canned peaches and maple syrup, blueberry syrup, or hot sugared strawberries.

Southwest Alaska

- Dillingham

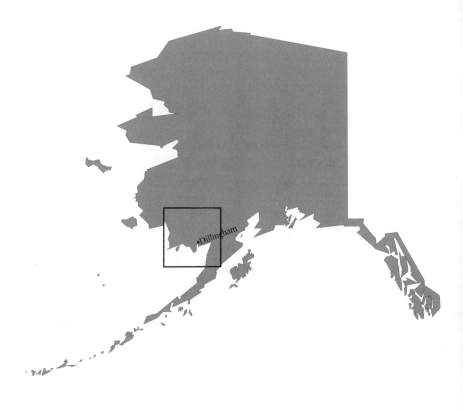

Southwest Alaska

Southwest Alaska comprises the Yukon-Kuskokwim Delta and the Bristol Bay region, considered by many to be Alaska's richest fishery. Fish caught commercially in this region include all five species of Pacific salmon, herring, halibut, Pacific cod, sablefish, pollock, mackerel, flounder, rockfish, crab and other shellfish. The region's many lakes and rivers are an angler's paradise, offering great fishing for salmon, rainbow trout, arctic char, grayling, northern pike, lake trout and Dolly Varden.

Beluga whales, orcas, walrus and seals frequent the offshore waters, while caribou, moose, bear, beaver, porcupine, otter, and fox wander the land. The area is the breeding ground for thousands of migratory waterfowl.

Togiak National Wildlife Refuge, located between Kuskokwim and Bristol Bay, is a primary breeding and resting spot for waterfowl and shorebirds that winter in Russia, Japan, Mexico, South America, New Zealand and the South Pacific. The more than 1,500 miles of salmon-spawning streams and rivers attract sport fishermen from all over the world. More information about the refuge is available by contacting: Refuge Manager Togiak National Wildlife Refuge, P.O. Box 270, Dillingham, AK 99576, phone (907) 842-1063, fax (907) 842-5402, e-mail togiak@fws.gov.

The State of Alaska has its own jewel in Wood-Tikchik State Park. Created in 1978, the 1.6-million-acre park is the largest state park in the nation. The park was named for its two separate, but connected clear-water lake systems. The fabulous fishing is a tremendous lure for anglers seeking a true wilderness experience. It is Alaska at its best. The state maintains few facilities in the park, but there are several private lodges within the boundaries, and air charters are available to take people in and out of the park. For more information about the park, contact Wood-Tikchik State Park, 550 W. 7th Ave., Suite 1390, Anchorage, AK 99501-3561, phone (907) 269-8698, or access their web site at www.dnr.state.ak.us/parks/units/woodtik.htm.

Dillingham

Dillingham is located about 350 air miles southwest of Anchorage. There are no roads leading here. Flight time is about one hour from Anchorage.

Located on the shores of Bristol Bay, with only 2,000 year-round residents, Dillingham is considered a rural or "bush" town. Folks in Dillingham tout their town as "Nature's Front Porch!" and, in fact, most visitors to Dillingham are passing through, on their way to remote hunting or fishing camps, or float trips down the Wood or Nushagak Rivers. It is the jumping off place for Wood-Tikchik State Park and is near the Togiak National Wildlife Refuge. Increasingly, however, visitors are spending more time in Dillingham, either on their way to or home from their other activities.

Dillingham traces its beginnings to pre-contact days, when the region was inhabited by by Yup'ik Eskimos and Athabaskans. The Russians established a trading post here in 1822, and a Russian Orthodox mission was established here in 1837, when the town became known as Nushagak. After the U.S. purchased Alaska from the Russians in 1867, it took nearly 20 years before Americans realized the potential worth of this portion of their new territory. In 1884, the first salmon cannery in the region was built just east of modern-day Dillingham. The townsite was first surveyed in 1947.

Among Dillingham's attractions are:

☒ *Samuel K. Fox Museum* — Named for a local, nationally known artist, this museum displays many examples of the diverse cultures that have inhabited the area.

☒ *Nushagak King Salmon Derby* — This is a summer competition for sports fishermen, with a monetary prize going to the one who catches the biggest king salmon. In 2000, the prize was $5,000.

☒ *Sled Dog Races* — In February, the middle-distance Nushagak Classic and the sprint Western Alaska Sled Dog Championship are held. The sprints are only one part of the Beaver Round Up Festival, Dillingham's winter carnival, another favorite event.

For more information, contact the Dillingham Chamber of Commerce at P.O. Box 348, Dillingham, AK 99576, (907) 842-5115, fax (907) 842-4097, e-mail dlgchmbr@nushtel.com

BEAVER CREEK BED & BREAKFAST

P. O. Box 563
1800 Birch Circle
Dillingham, AK 99576
(907) 842-5500 weekdays, (907) 842-5366 eves & weekends
Fax (907) 842-5938
E-mail: isaacsne@nushtel.com
Web Site: www.dillinghamalaska.com
Susan and Gorden Isaacs, Hosts

Months Open: Year round   **Children Welcome:** Yes
Hours: **Pets Accommodated:** Inquire
Credit Cards: MC, VISA, AMEX, DS   **Social Drinking:** Yes
Accommodations: 4 rooms, 1 cottage,   **Smoking:** No
    1 private house

ROOM RATES
Single: $100
Double: $130-$140
(Please add 10% bed tax to all rates)

This beautiful three-story bed & breakfast is a spacious 4,800 square feet, of which 2,000 square feet are dedicated to the guest area. The guest area is downstairs and feature a large seating area, with large windows facing south, overlooking a meandering creek, populated by beavers. Black spruce and birch trees surround the property. The guest area, which has its

own private kitchen, is furnished with couches, rocker, big-screen TV with cable and VCR, private telephone line and answering machine.

Two of the bedrooms, one with a queen-size bed and one with two twin beds, have a vanity sink in room, but share a bath. The other room in this area has two queen-size beds and a private bath/shower in the room. The fourth bedroom is on the main floor of the house. It has a queen-size bed and a twin bed, its own TV, a vanity with a sink in room and a private bathroom.

The private guest cottage can accommodate up to four people. It has a loft bedroom with two twin beds and a queen-size bed and queen-size hideabed downstairs. A kitchen and bath make up the rest of the cottage. It has cable TV and VCR, as well as a private telephone and answering machine, and a washer and dryer.

The *Trail House* is a private, two-bedroom house which will sleep up to five people. It has four twin beds and a queen-size bed. A kitchen, living room and bath make up the rest of the house. It has cable TV and VCR, private telephone with answering machine.

Breakfast in both the main house and the cottage is self serve. Fruit, juice and muffins are set out. Coffee is hot and ready upon awaking. Hot teas and hot chocolates are available. Cereal, eggs, bacon, yogurt, bread and other items are available for those wanting a bigger breakfast. Special dietary needs will be met.

A special feature of the B&B is the Maqi, or Alaska sauna, located on the property. The wood-fired steam room features two 8 by 10 rooms and is a wonderful place to relax and unwind from the day's activities.

Gordon Isaacs is a 26-year resident of Dillingham. A licensed general contractor, he also owns a building supply store. Susan, a 11-year resident of the town, manages the B&B and works at the store. Their two adopted girls love meeting people and showing them around the property. The family shares its home with an outside dog named Shaggy.

The Isaacs' provide airport pickup and returns and may, upon request, take guests downtown. In addition, they offer much information about the area and can help plan your trip, assisting with sightseeing tours, fishing and hunting camps and one-day fishing trips. "Our goal is to make every visitor leave with a smile on their face after a positive bush experience," they say.

beaver

More Recipes
From Your
Bed & Breakfast Hosts

APRICOT KUGEL

1 c. dried apricots
1/2 c. apricot preserves
1/2 c. butter
12-oz pkg. wide egg noodles

1/4 c. sugar
2 c. sour cream
5 eggs

Preheat oven to 350°. Place apricots in medium saucepan and cover with water. Bring to a boil and simmer 10 minutes or until soft. Drain any remaining water. Mix in apricot preserves; set aside. Prepare noodles; drain. While noodles are cooking, cut butter into 10 pieces and place in large bowl. Add hot, cooked noodles and stir until melted. Add sugar and sour cream; let cool. Beat eggs and add to mixture. Place in greased 9" x 13" glass baking dish. Spread apricot mixture on top. Bake at 350° for 1 hour.

— Leicha Welton, 7 Gables Inn

BLUEBERRY STUFFED FRENCH TOAST

12 slices French bread, cut into 1" cubes
2 3-oz. pkgs. cream cheese, chilled
  and cut into 1" cubes
1 c. fresh blueberries, rinsed & drained

6 large eggs
1/3 c. maple syrup
2 c. milk

Grease 13" x 9" baking pan. Place half of the bread cubes into the pan. Scatter cream cheese over the bread and sprinkle with blueberries. Top with remaining bread cubes. In a bowl, combine eggs, syrup and milk. Pour over bread mixture. Cover and chill overnight. Bake at 350° covered with foil for 30 minutes, then remove foil and continue baking for 30 minutes. Serve with Blueberry Syrup.

BLUEBERRY SYRUP

1 c. sugar
2 T. cornstarch
1 c. water

1 c. fresh blueberries
1 T. butter

Combine first three ingredients in a saucepan. Cook for five minutes. Add blueberries and cook for another 10 minutes. Remove from heat and add butter.

— Judy Urquhart, Blueberry Lodge

BLUFF HOUSE CINNAMON ROLLS

Rolls:

1 pkg. yellow cake mix	butter
2 pkg. dry yeast	brown sugar
5 c. flour	cinnamon
2-1/2 c. warm water	nuts
1 T. salt	

Topping:

1 c. margarine	1-1/2 T. flour
1-1/2 c. brown sugar	4 T. milk

Topping — Melt margarine, stir in sugar, flour and milk. Spread in the bottom of two 9" x 13" pans. **Rolls** — Combine cake mix, yeast, flour, water and salt. Put in greased bowl and let rise. Roll out; spread dough with butter and sprinkle with mixture of brown sugar, cinnamon and nuts. Roll up; cut into slices and place on topping in pans. Let rise and bake at 350° until golden brown, about 35 minutes.

— Margie Smith, Bluff House Bed & Breakfast

BREAD-MAKER CINNAMON ROLLS, SITKA STYLE

1/4 c. water	1 tsp. salt
1 egg, beaten	butter, softened
3 c. flour	2 tsp. cinnamon
6 T. sugar	1/2 c. sugar
2 T. powdered milk	raisins
1-1/2 to 2 tsp. rapid-rise yeast	half and half

Place water and egg in automatic bread-maker bucket. Add the next five ingredients, in order listed. Return bucket to maker and select "dough" setting. When beeper signals dough is ready, roll dough out. Spread with softened butter, then sprinkle with mixture of cinnamon and sugar and raisins. Roll up and cut into desired thickness and quantity. Place rolls in buttered 9" x 13" baking pan sprinkled with brown sugar. Cover and set aside to rise overnight. Next morning, pour a little half-and-half around the rolls, just enough to cover the brown sugar. Bake at 350° for 30 minutes. Drizzle with powdered sugar blended with vanilla and a little milk. The brown sugar and half-and-half make a light caramel.

— Carole Denkinger, Alaska Ocean View Bed & Breakfast

BUTTERMILK PANCAKES

1 c. buttermilk	pinch of mace
1 egg	1 tsp. baking soda
1/2 c. flour	1/4-1/2 c. fresh blueberries

Whisk together milk, egg, soda and mace. Add flour. Mix in blueberries (can substitute thawed, drained frozen berries for fresh). Preheat griddle until drop of water sizzles. Drop batter by tablespoonfuls onto griddle. Turn when golden. Serve with whipped butter and pure maple syrup.

This recipe can be doubled, tripled, etc. for large crowds. The batter is thin like crepes and makes very light and tender pancakes.

— Susan Lutz, The Oscar Gill House

CINNAMON RAISIN FRENCH TOAST

8 eggs	1/2 c. brown sugar
1-1/2 c. milk	2 T. butter
1/2 c. half and half	1/2 c. maple syrup
1 tsp. vanilla	cinnamon
12 slices cinnamon-raisin bread	

Melt butter in bottom of 9"x13" baking pan. When melted, spread brown sugar over bottom of pan. Mix together eggs, milk and vanilla. Place 6 slices of bread on top of brown sugar and pour part of the egg mixture over bread. Sprinkle with cinnamon. Place the remaining 6 slices of bread on top and pour remaining egg mixture over all. Sprinkle with cinnamon. Cover and refrigerate overnight. In the morning, remove from refrigerator and let stand at room temperature while oven is heating to 350°. Pour syrup over bread mixture. Bake for 45 minutes. More syrup can be added after it's cooled.

— Kathy Huston, Alaskan Host Bed & Breakfast

FRESH FRUIT BREAKFAST PARFAIT

1 c. plain yogurt	2 c. fresh berries
1 c. homemade granola	2 kiwi fruits
2 T. honey	whipped cream

Layer all ingredients in parfait glasses. top with whipped cream and a fresh mint leaf. Serves 4.

— Judy Swanson, Swan House Bed & Breakfast

ELDERBERRY B&B BELGIAN WAFFLES

1 c. butter or margarine   1/8 tsp. baking powder
1-1/2 c. sugar   1/8 tsp. salt
2 eggs   1 tsp. grated lemon rind
2 tsp. vanilla   2-1/2 c. water

Cream butter, sugar, eggs and vanilla. Add remaining ingredients and blend until smooth. Bake in hot waffle iron until done.

— Linda Seitz, Elderberry Bed & Breakfast

FRENCH HOT CHOCOLATE

1/3 c. semisweet chocolate pieces   1/2 tsp. vanilla
1/4 c. light corn syrup   1 c. chilled whipping cream
3 T. water   4 c. milk

Heat chocolate pieces, corn syrup and water over low heat in small pan, stirring until chocolate is melted and mixture is smooth. Stir in vanilla and chill. In chilled bowl, beat cream until stiff, adding chocolate mixture gradually. Beat until mixture mounds when dropped from spoon. Heat milk until warm. Fill cups half full with cream mixture. Fill cups with warm milk and mix. Serve immediately.

— Leicha Welton, 7 Gables Inn

GREEN CHILI EGG CASSEROLE

Sourdough or French bread   Splash of Tabasco
7 eggs   2 small cloves pressed garlic
2¹/2 c. milk (2% OK)   or 1/2 tsp. powdered
1 tsp. oregano   4-5 c. grated Monterey Jack
4-oz. can chopped Ortega chiles   & cheddar cheese

Oil 9"x13" pan and cover bottom with sourdough or French bread slices (day old is fine). Whisk remainder of ingredients together and pour over bread slices. Cover with cheese. Cover tightly and refrigerate overnight. Bake at 325° for 1 hour. Serve hot with fresh salsa, chopped scallions, yogurt or sour cream, and avocado slices. Goes very well with cornmeal biscuits or muffins and cherry jam.

— Susan Lutz, The Oscar Gill House

HALIBUT OLYMPIA

Halibut fillets (fresh or frozen) Parmesan cheese
Mayonnaise   Garlic
Dijon mustard   Onions, sliced

Mix mayonnaise and mustard to desired tanginess. Add cheese and garlic. Spread mixture over fillets (a 1/4" layer is preferred). Place halibut in baking pan on a bed of raw onions. Sprinkle bread crumbs over top of fish. Bake at 350° until top is brown and fish flakes easily.

— Carole Denkinger, Alaska Ocean View Bed & Breakfast

MJ'S SEAFOOD STEW

1/2 c. cooking sherry or whiskey   1 c. chopped celery
1/2 c. Worcestershire sauce   1/2 lb. fresh mushrooms,
1/2 lb. seafood (halibut, rockfish,   sliced
    cod or scallops) cut in 1" cubes 2 T. sage (or more)
1 lb. shrimp   6 oz. can tomatoes, cut up
1/2 tsp. cayenne pepper   16 oz. can tomato paste
1 lg. green pepper, cut in strips   2¹/₂ c. water
3/4 c. chopped green or white onion 1 T. oregano (or more)
Salt to taste

Place seafood in a single layer in a shallow pan. Combine sherry, Worcestershire sauce and cayenne. Pour over seafood to coat. Marinate for 3-4 hours in the refrigerator. Drain seafood and save marinade. In a Dutch oven or large pot, saute peppers, onions and mushrooms. Add celery, tomatoes, water, marinade, sage and oregano. Bring to boil. Reduce heat and cook uncovered for 30 minutes, or until reduced by half. Add seafood and continue to cook for 10-15 minutes. Be careful not to overcook the seafood.

Serve with one scoop of cooked rice in the bottom of a bowl, hearty bread and a green salad. Serves 6.

— Mary Jane Lastufka, Across the Bay Tent & Breakfast

OPEN-FACE HOT HALIBUT SANDWICH

Boneless, skinless halibut
Garlic
Tiger Sauce

Cream cheese
French bread, sliced
Cheddar or parmesan cheese

Cook halibut and garlic in covered skillet until fish flakes. Break fish apart and cool to near room temperature. Mix fish with commercial Tiger Sauce and room-temperature cream cheese. Spread mixture on sliced French bread. Top with grated cheddar or parmesan cheese and broil until cheese melts. You may add minced green onions to the spread, if you desire.

— Carole Denkinger, Alaska Ocean View Bed & Breakfast

POACHED FISH FILLETS

Fillets
Halibut fillets, split down center*
1/2 c. milk
1/2 c. water
1/4 tsp. white pepper
Parsley for garnish
* If fillets are too thick to roll, cut
in half horizontally, then split

Shrimp Sauce
1/3 c. butter
1/3 c. flour
1 1/2 qts. half-n-half
1 1/2 tsp. paprika
2 tsp. salt
1 c. canned mushrooms
1 lb. cooked small shrimp

Fillets: Starting with wide end, roll fillets and fasten with a toothpick. Place halibut rolls into large skillet and add milk, water and pepper. Cover tightly and simmer gently for 10 minutes. Remove to hot platter and remove toothpicks. Cover with Shrimp Sauce and garnish with parsley.

Shrimp Sauce: Place first three ingredients in top of double boiler and cook over hot water, stirring frequently, until thickened. Add rest of ingredients. Pour over halibut fillets.

— Carole Denkinger, Alaska Ocean View Bed & Breakfast

PORCUPINE SALMON

Batter:
Bisquick and beer to desired thickness or
Krusteaz Buttermilk mix and beer to desired thickness
1 c. coconut

Mix batter, making sure it is not too thin, or it will not stick to the fish. Cube salmon. Dip in batter and deep fry. Serve with sweet and sour sauce. UMMMM good! Serve with rice or baked potato, green salad, jello salad, garlic bread or toast and anything else you like!

— Luanne Cottle, Emerald Isle Bed & Breakfast

POTATO PANCAKES

4 c. grated raw potatoes	1/4 c. flour
3 eggs	1/4 c. onion, chopped fine
1 tsp. salt	dash of pepper

Mix all ingredients and fry like regular pancakes, oiling the griddle before each pancake is placed in pan. Serve with—

Creamed Bacon Gravy: Fry 1 lb. bacon. Pour off grease and set bacon aside to serve with pancakes. Place 2 T. bacon grease back into pan. Mix in 3 T. flour, 3 T. cold water, dash of pepper, ¹/2 tsp. Italian seasoning. Add 1 can evaporated milk (low fat OK). Turn burner on medium heat and stir mixture constantly until boiling. Add more water if gravy is too thick.

— Fran Latham, The Blue Heron Inn

SEAFOOD BREAKFAST CREPES WITH HOLLANDAISE

Crepes:
In a blender, mix: 1 c. milk, 1 c. flour, pinch of salt, 4 eggs. Place batter in covered bowl in refrigerator and let set at least 1 hour or overnight. When ready to prepare, remove batter from refrigerator and pulse once or twice to stir. Do not overmix. Coat bottom of a cast iron skillet or crepe pan with butter and place over medium-high heat. Pour 2-3 T. of batter into hot pan; tilt and rotate pan to coat entire bottom. When set and slightly golden brown, turn and cook other side briefly. Place crepes on a warm plate, separating each crepe with a paper towel. Cover to keep warm and pliable and set aside.

Filling:
In a large frying pan, saute until transluscent one chopped medium onion. Transfer to a bowl, cover to keep warm, and set aside. If desired, saute additional ingredients such as chopped, seeded Roma tomatoes, yellow, red, orange or green peppers. Set aside to keep warm.

In a separate frying pan, prepare scrambled eggs in butter. Use 1 to 1-1/2 eggs per person. Cover and set aside.

In a large frying pan, melt butter with a little oil and saute until opaque 1 lb. halibut cut into small cubes. Do not overcook! Drain off excess liquid. Gently stir into fish in pan the onions and other sauted vegetables, the eggs, chopped chives or minced green onion tops, 2 c. grated pepper jack cheese, 1 T. rinsed capers or 2-4 T. salsa, lemon pepper and salt to taste. Cover and set aside.

Warm the stack of crepes in microwave for 1 minute. Place about 1/2 c. fish mixture in a line across each crepe, an inch or two from center line, roll crepe, leaving ends open. Place seam side down on heated serving platter. Allow 2 crepes per serving. Cover with warm damp towel and set in warm oven while preparing sauce.

Hollandaise Sauce:
Place 3 eggs in bowl of hot tap water for several minutes. Separate eggs and mix yolks in blender with 1 T. warm lemon juice and 1 T. hot water, pinch of cayenne pepper and pinch of salt. Cover and process on high 3 seconds. In a steady stream, slowly add 1/2 c. melted butter (not browned). Serve sauce at once or keep warm by setting blender in pan of very warm water.

Pour sauce over filled, rolled crepes. Sprinkle with chopped chives and a little grated pepper jack cheese and serve immediately. Pass extra sauce.

— Carole Denkinger, Alaska Ocean View B&B

THE GABLES FRITTATA

1/2 lb. sausage
2 green onions, chopped
2 c. shredded zucchini
1/2 c. whipping cream
6 eggs
1 c. shredded mozzarella cheese

1/2 tsp. oregano
1/2 tsp. basil
1 T. dry Italian salad dressing mix
4 oz. cream cheese, softened
1 c. shredded cheddar cheese

Brown sausage and drain on paper towel. Place the sausage in an 8" quiche pan or pie plate. Spread zucchini and onions over the sausage and sprinkle with the seasonings. Beat the eggs with the whipping cream and pour over zucchini and sausage. Cut the cream cheese into cubes and sprinkle evenly over the top. Cover with mozzarella and cheddar cheese. Bake at 325° for 45 minutes or until set. Serves 6.

— Leicha Welton, 7 Gables Inn

WALKABOUT TOWN RHUBARB SYRUP

6 c. rhubarb, washed and cut
     into 1" cubes

6 c. sugar
1 T. cinnamon

Bring sugar, cinnamon and rhubarb to a boil. Boil for 10 minutes. Cool and strain the syrup. Syrup is wonderful on pancakes, waffles, ice cream, etc. The rhubarb which is left after straining can be added to muffins as a tasty, high-fiber ingredient.

— Sandra Stimson, Walkabout Town Bed & Breakfast

Indexes

LISTING REQUEST FORM

If you would like to have your Bed And Breakfast included in future editions of *Bed And Breakfast Alaska Style!*, please send us your name and address and we will send you a questionnaire the next time the book is updated. There is a fee for listing.

YOUR NAME_____

B&B NAME_____

ADDRESS_____

CITY/STATE/ZIP_____

MAIL THIS FORM TO:

WIZARD WORKS
P.O. Box 1125
Homer, AK 99603

--------------------------------CLIP HERE--------------------------------

LISTING REQUEST FORM

If you would like to have your Bed And Breakfast included in future editions of *Bed And Breakfast Alaska Style!*, please send us your name and address and we will send you a questionnaire the next time the book is updated. There is a fee for listing.

YOUR NAME_____

B&B NAME_____

ADDRESS_____

CITY/STATE/ZIP_____

MAIL THIS FORM TO:

WIZARD WORKS
P.O. Box 1125
Homer, AK 99603

ORDER FORM

Please send me _____ copies of *Bed & Breakfast Alaska Style!* For each copy, I am enclosing $16.95, plus postage and handling of $3 for the first book ordered and $.50 for each additional book.

TOTAL NUMBER OF BOOKS ORDERED_____
TOTAL AMOUNT ENCLOSED: $_____

YOUR NAME_____

ADDRESS_____ _____ _

CITY/STATE/ZIP _____

I prefer to pay by MC/VISA _ _ _ _   _ _ _ _   _ _ _ _   _ _ _ _   Exp._____

MAIL THIS FORM WITH PAYMENT TO:
WIZARD WORKS
P.O. Box 1125
Homer, AK 99603
or Fax to: (907) 235-8757

---CLIP HERE---

ORDER FORM

Please send me _____ copies of *Bed & Breakfast Alaska Style!* For each copy, I am enclosing $16.95, plus postage and handling of $3 for the first book ordered and $.50 for each additional book.

TOTAL NUMBER OF BOOKS ORDERED_____
TOTAL AMOUNT ENCLOSED: $_____

YOUR NAME_____

ADDRESS_____

CITY/STATE/ZIP _____

I prefer to pay by MC/VISA _ _ _ _   _ _ _ _   _ _ _ _   _ _ _ _   Exp._____

MAIL THIS FORM WITH PAYMENT TO:
WIZARD WORKS
P.O. Box 1125
Homer, AK 99603
or Fax to (907) 235-8757